Modern Dance

Modern Dance

GAY CHENEY

Associate Professor of
Physical Education,
California State College at Hayward

JANET STRADER

Henry Street Playhouse,
New York City

ALLYN AND BACON, Inc.   **Boston**

Library of Congress Catalog Card Number: 69–17383

Printed in the United States of America.

Second printing . . . October, 1971

Foreword

SPORTS AND OTHER forms of physical activity are an important part of our culture. Recognizing this, Allyn and Bacon has published this distinctive series of books on the basic concepts of a number of physical activities. These books represent a high point in both curriculum design and instructional materials.

The *conceptual approach* has been used in the development of these books. This approach starts with the identification of the *key concepts* around which the activity is structured. These statements, and the sub-concepts which support them, serve as the basis for organizing and relating the facts and skills of the activity into a meaningful whole. The learner is guided in developing these cognitive and motor concepts through a series of *learning experiences*. These experiences are designed to involve him in the learning process, both intellectually and physically.

Although these books are designed primarily to be used as supplements to instructional classes, their unique structure and clear presentation can enable a student to learn the activity even without the direction of a teacher if necessary.

The authors have been selected on a national scale. All have excellent backgrounds as performers and teachers in their fields. The combination of these high calibre people and the conceptual organization of the material has produced a series of books which will be of great value in improving instruction in physical education.

Thomas W. Evaul, Temple University
Raymond A. Snyder, University of California

v

Preface

A GUIDEBOOK, SAYS the dictionary, is a handbook of information for travelers. This guidebook is for you who are about to do some of the most fascinating traveling in the world.

For dance *is* traveling; dance is going; dance is movement; dance is motion. What distinguishes dance from other kinds of travel is its emphasis on the manner of going. Dance is concerned not with the gross act of getting from one place to another, but with the nature of its itineraries.

The traveler's experiences along the way shape the character of his journey. The student of dance has countless experiences which shape the course of his study. In fact, experiencing dance is the only way to know it. No one can merely read a book and become a dancer. This book is not meant to suggest that, nor does it advocate that you substitute the guidebook for the guide. There is no substitute for a fine teacher.

Rather, this book maps out a pattern of experiences the student dancer might have. It is meant to be read in motion. Like the traveler, the dance student can make what he wishes of those experiences. And if, like the traveler, he comes home broadened by his journey, with his thirst for travel not quenched, but increased, with memories of the going alive in his mind and body—then he will know what it is to have danced.

Gay Cheney
Janet Strader

Contents

Concept I—Modern Dance Is an Experience in Movement

1. Movement enables you to know your world.

THIS BOOK IS about modern dance and also about you. The importance of our subject is the relationship between you and movement. As you know, the beginning of life is movement and the end of life stops movement forever. Most of your basic knowledges came to you through movement. You first experienced yourself by the movement of your body. You first experienced your environment and other people by moving in relation to them. Feelings of satisfaction, frustration, love, fear and pain were experienced through subtle changes of the body in movement. Concepts of space, time and energy were learned as they related to your motion. You discovered the forces of gravity and momentum by having to move with and against them. Your first and last reactions to life, situations and people are in the form of movement. This rich background should make dance a most natural activity for you. Many times, however, you may have developed attitudes about your body and movement that allowed you to let your movement awareness slip and to get out of practice using your own body. It is hoped that this book will remind you of this natural process.

You know many things through your body, from the many different life experiences which are registered in your muscles as memories. You know in your body what it is like to be in a crowd, to be in a hurry or in hesitation, in fear or joy, in a hammock or on the floor, in sunlight or shade. You know what it's like to be excited in the quivering of your knees, the quickness of your heartbeat, the busyness of your hands with each other. And you will know many other things through the feelings of your body, in the experiences yet to come. You will know your body in new ways, in new shapes and rhythms, in new tensions and energies. You will find yourself in new amounts of space, in new relationships with other people, with things, with lights, with shapes and textures. Whatever you experience, do it with your *entire* self, with your eyes and skin, mind and body, breathing and swallowing. Register each experience in your memory, and use it in the future with reference to your dances and your own further definition.

Dance is movement. Movement is life, and it surrounds you every moment. It attracts your attention in the form of flashing neon lights on busy streets, kinetic sculptures in museums or rotating advertisements in shop windows. It fascinates you with animals, other people, racing rivers and tangled traffic. You exist by means of it every day, from the earliest rising out of bed to the last flick of the light switch at night. Being alive means moving, and movement is the material of dance.

LEARNING EXPERIENCE
Think of three things you learned (really understood, not just memorized) in the last year. What role did movement play in learning these?

---

2. The uniqueness of your body provides you with certain feelings about moving.

In many ways you are all alike. You have bodies with approximately the standard number of parts. You all have a shape, weight, height, size and width. You have a torso, hips, shoulders, front and back. You possess arms and legs, knees and elbows, hands and feet, eyes and nose—even *these* will dance.

The particular shape, size, weight and height of your body—all the parts together—are what provide you with your individuality. This constitution is *yours*. There is none other quite like it in all the world. You need not be concerned with evaluating it in comparison with others or with any standard of perfection. It is sufficient to know that your body is different; what makes it different and unique makes up the quality of you. Know yourself realistically. Accept whatever part of yourself is unchangeable. You are not better or worse than, but taller, shorter, rounder, more muscular, longer legged, heavier thighed, wider footed, shorter nosed than other people. You will know much more about yourself and the possibilities of your particular body as you go along.

3. Your body is you, and your realization of it is important.

Your uniqueness gives you certain feelings about movement and certain preferences. Some movements you find boring, only routine, while others you find quite satisfying, even exciting. You may feel at home in the hustle-bustle of a city, or you may prefer to sit and watch the subtle motion of change in the panorama of a sunset. You may feel at your best when engaged in vigorous action, or you may seldom move. You may like to run and jump, fall and rise; or you may enjoy merely changing the expression on your face. After discovering your own likes and dislikes, comforts and discomforts in movement, you will explore new possibilities in motion and discover many new likes and meanings, extend the range of what is comfortable for you, so that the possibilities for your choreography become greater.

LEARNING EXPERIENCE
Compare yourself with a close friend. How are you physically, emotionally, intellectually and socially different and alike? Observe his movement. How do you differ in this respect? How are you similar? Can you identify any characteristics about him that seem to influence his movement? About yourself?

---

4. Dance enables you to explore and understand space, time and energy.

The elements of dance have to do with the way energy is expended and the way time and space are used. You are always influenced by these abstract elements in everyday living, although you may not be consciously aware of it and of your reaction to it.

You have feelings about space and about yourself in space. You may feel cozy in a corner, or like to sit close to other people; or you may feel comfortable all curled up, in a place that is particularly yours. You may like lots of room, or like to experience different places in a room; you may feel hampered by crowds and penned up in subways. You may go in a single direction, or you may like to wander, trying many new paths. Some people go constantly around in circles.

You are sensitive to things outside yourself in space. You may be thrilled by the height of a skyscraper jutting into the sky, or you may like the soft curves of rolling hills. You may laugh at squat, round shapes, or be threatened by square corners. You may feel that angles are exciting, or that off-balances are intriguing. You will make use of these sensitivities and awarenesses in your dances, and perhaps in your use of the stage.

Then, too, you will develop responses to other people's use of space. You may react in a certain way to a person who seems absolutely open and unprotected, and in another way toward one who keeps his arms and legs tightly crossed, tapping only one finger. You know this other person because of the way he is in space.

In dance, you will have new spatial experiences. You will try to simulate curves in all parts of your body, make your legs appear longer, your knees round. You will condense space and expand it, perhaps break it up, but never ignore it.

Time is another element with which you are concerned daily—by watch, bell or bus schedule. It makes you hurry, allows you to be lazy or may cause anxiety. Time is continuous; it goes on regardless of what you do. You can go with it or against it; you can get caught up in the hurry or drift along slowly. You may know yourself as one who enjoys running with your motor revved up, making sudden starts and stops and being excited by an unexpected change. On the other hand, you may be one who likes slowness, who is secure in the expected and lulled by routine.

You know time already, and will know it better as you progress in dance. You will discover new slowness and fastness, the effect of continuity and of contrast, and the sense of time passing. You will become aware of the rhythm of breathing, of feeling and of motion. You will move in, with and through time, and will use it in brand new ways.

Dance uses energy carefully and meaningfully. You do this every day—you use energy to accomplish what you set out to do. You know yourself in relation to energy, as well as in time and space. There are times when you abound in it, being explosive and volatile; other times you have little energy, being a droop and a drag. Perhaps you just use it carefully, in light and delicate ways. Your energy may be contained and ready for important things, always there just below the surface, popping into your eyes in a ready smile, making your mouth corners turn up, or perhaps turn down in a sudden outburst of temper. Your energy may be always there as tension, existing as a habit like coffee and cigarettes. That which you sense as energy has a lot to do with what we call *personality*.

Energy is closely linked with time and space. Energy is necessary for one to move through space, and moving through space takes time. Each element is affected by all the others. If you must hurry to go somewhere far away, tension accumulates. If you have lots of time and nowhere to go, energy may be held in reserve.

Energy is carefully defined in dance. Movement can be accomplished only by its expenditure, and will be qualified by the way in which it is expended. It can be dissected into vibrations per second, exploded in short sharp bursts, or used to help you resist the temptation to give in and collapse. You will know energy, how to generate it and how and where to spend it. Movement will require it; the idea will require it; your energy will command them both.

Movement in dance, then, will include articulation of all these elements at once, in the same way that they always exist simultaneously. Space, time and energy are your raw materials. They are what dance is about.

LEARNING EXPERIENCE
Does all movement involve energy, time and space? As you move in your daily life, concentrate on each of these aspects one at a time, trying to become more aware of them. Watch for them in the movement of others.

---

5. Dance training includes experiences in technique, moving through space, improvisation, choreography and performance.

In your encounter with dance, each experience will be a new one. Even if you were presented with the same motional problem a thousand times, you would find a thousand different ways to solve it. The reasons are, of course, that the possibilities for human movement are nearly limitless, and you are never the same person you were when you solved the problem the first time or the second or the twenty-seventh.

Your experiences in dance training will probably fall into five general areas: technique, moving through space, spontaneous invention, choreography and performance. You will not necessarily work with them in that order, as they are not sequentially related. You may work in all five areas in a single day's class. The experiences in this book have been chosen to give you a variety of new sensations in motion and a number of different approaches to your own creative resources. Since these experiences will not necessarily happen chronologically, this book does not recommend a particular order of events. You may prefer to skip around and read what is pertinent to you at each stage of your own development.

Most dance classes begin with a period of *technique*, the purpose of which is to warm up the body and to practice those daily rituals which will stretch it, strengthen it and make it a responsive tool with which to work. Following this, there may be a period of *moving through space*, quite a different sensation from moving in one place. Often this will consist of a movement combination presented by your instructor as a means for you to work on some particular principle of motion. The combination, in itself, is not the important thing; the point of view *is*. It is just like algebra: once you understand the principle, you can solve any problem.

Creative dance has nothing to do with imitating movement patterns or learning combinations for their own sake. You will spend much of your time in spontaneous invention, discovering movement and creating patterns for yourself. This is the greatest fun of all, as there is unlimited material from which to draw. Anyone and everyone can invent. In this book you will find experiences in which you are asked to *explore* a particular area of movement. By this, it is meant that you should try many solutions to the problem, stopping, starting, going back and trying another. It is an exhaustive type of search, narrowly focused within certain limitations. When you *improvise*, you move spontaneously, letting one movement lead into the next. You try not to stop or break the flow of movement associations. You may start out searching for a specific kind of movement, but may discover that the search has led you to something far more interesting. You keep right on going, wherever the improvisation leads you. Improvisation is less strictly channeled than exploration, and is continuous in time from beginning to end.

From your experiences in motion you will *choreograph* your own studies and dances. You will find movement or idea materials through the processes of exploration and improvisation in the same way that you discover new ideas through occasional spontaneous, unplanned or uncalculated responses. You will shape these discovered materials into some final form as a dance in the same way that you order your thoughts in certain organizations. While these kinds of thoughts are concerned with words, dance is concerned with motion, or with particular sensed thoughts or feelings that are as yet beyond words, nonverbal. In dance you will organize shapes, rhythms, dynamics and movement ideas.

You organize your thoughts in order to communicate them to others by writing or speaking them. You will be forming movement for the same ultimate purpose—for sharing the form with others. After all, even though it may be very satisfying simply to have a new idea or a fresh solution to a problem, the maximum pleasure comes in telling someone else about it. When your dance is exciting and meaningful to you, you will want others to see it. Your dances will not be large-scale epics at this stage of the game, but they will afford you additional opportunities to solidify your movement experience.

You will *perform.* You will perform for and with your class, for your instructor, for friends and for strangers. You will perform not only choreographies but every small part of every exercise, of every step across the floor and of every improvisation. Performance is not just "dancing the dance." It is being present and being supremely aware in each motion and moment. Performance sounds a little frightening, perhaps, but when you consider that you present yourself to many people in many situations every day, it is a quite natural occurrence. It is spine-tingling because it occurs in that coveted and, at the same time, fearsome center of attention. It will be most meaningful as an experience if you have something of value to offer while you are there. The book has this end in mind.

LEARNING EXPERIENCE
Observe a modern dancer, teacher or an advanced class. Can you classify each of the activities you observe into one of the five training areas? What do you view as the ultimate experience in dance?

Concept II—The Body Instrument Requires Intelligent Cultivation and Tuning for Dance

THE WORKING TOOL of the violinist is his instrument, the painter his brush, and the dancer his body. So pick up your instrument and begin. Your body demands that you treat it with intelligence, awareness, sensitivity, discipline and kindness. You will live both inside and outside your body, so as to see, as well as feel, what is going on.

You will experience your body as a whole and also in its separate parts. Nearly everyone knows his nose from his toes, and has since earliest childhood, so a discussion of the parts of the body may seem superfluous. In dance, however, there are certain parts that need specific attention. These need to be clarified, so that you will speak not of the back, but of the lower, middle or upper spine, and not of the hip bone when you really mean the hip joint.

1. An understanding of the body parts and their movement potential makes more intelligent movement possible.

The spine is basic to all human movement. It is a long series of bones extending from the base of the head, at about ear level, to the coccyx, or tailbone. It consists of 24 separate bones, or vertebrae, and two others, the sacrum and coccyx—five separate vertebrae in infancy, but fused into one by adulthood.

The spine has natural curves in it—a forward curve at the neck, a backward curve at the ribs, another forward curve at the waist, and a backward curve below the waist. These curves are meant to be there, but are not meant to be exaggerated. Fluidity of motion in the spine is a desirable asset to the dancer, and many of the things you will be asked to do are designed to give more mobility to the spine by working the curves opposite to their normal direction.

For convenience, you can speak of the spine in three sections.

8

The *upper spine* extends from the base of the head to just below the shoulder blades. The *middle spine* continues from there to waist level, and the *lower spine* includes the remaining vertebrae, the sacrum and the coccyx. Each of these areas can be trained to operate independently of the others, or together as a totality.

LEARNING EXPERIENCE
Locate the three spinal areas on a friend, or on yourself in front of a mirror. Move them forward and back. Flex them. Extend them.

The area of the hips is often a confusing one. The *hip bones,* first of all, are the prominent bones found on the front of the body, about three inches below the waist and about shoulder width apart. The *hip joint* is where the leg is attached to the torso.

LEARNING EXPERIENCE
Put the heel of your hand on your hip bone and extend your fingers downward. Your palm will cross your hip joint. Lift your thigh forward and feel the break in your hip joint.

Later, when you read "hips forward," this is the part of your hip that is directed forward—the whole area you just covered with your hand. The *side of your hips* is at the same level as your hip joint and can be felt as prominent bones on the sides of your body.

LEARNING EXPERIENCE
Place your thumb at your waist and stretch your middle finger down the side of your body. It will reach the area known as the side of the hip. Let your weight sink into one hip, and you will easily find this area.

Further on, when you read of moving your hips in a backward direction, this means that the whole lower spine area is moving backward, not just the tip of your spine. Moving only the tip of your spine will cause your pelvis to tilt, exaggerating the curve at your waist in the well-known "swayback" posture; this is to be avoided in most cases.

One other important body part is the *sternum,* or breastbone. This is, for the dancer, the focal point of the chest and a key to much of the dancer's movement. A lifted sternum exudes confidence; a sunken sternum suggests timidity, fatigue and laziness. The sternum is also important in balance. Its placement over the ball of the foot means stability when standing, moving or balancing on one foot.

LEARNING EXPERIENCE
Practice lifting the sternum and letting it sink. Observe the effect in the mirror. Note the resultant feeling in your muscles and joints.

The rest of the body terminology used in dance is much the same as you have learned from childhood.

(In many of the following experiences, you will be asked to improvise and choreograph. You might find it helpful to read Concepts IV and V now, and again later as you progress. Understanding more and more about improvisation and choreography will make your experiences with them that much richer. Conversely, the more experiences you have in these areas, the greater will be your understanding of the material in this book.)

LEARNING EXPERIENCES
Explore the parts of your body individually. Choose a hand, shoulder, head, hips or any other part. Discover what its possibilities for movement are, then use it to initiate movement of your whole body. Move several parts in a sequence. Move one part while moving another in the same way, then in a contrasting way.

Improvise with body parts, projecting each particular part more strongly than you project the total body. By your own attention to them, make the viewer see just your head, your knee or your elbow.

Explore the possibilities for movement with two parts of the body connected: an elbow to a knee, a hand to a foot or both hands joined behind the neck. Try the same problem with another person, moving head to head, hand to foot, back to back or shoulder to hip.

Improvise with one or more people, relating your movement to theirs. Choose the same body parts or different ones. Find that delicate balance of movement relationship in which you are subtly influenced by each other's motion, without either of you imitating or dominating the other.

---

2. The action possible for each joint determines the movement available for dance.

Before reading about the body in motion, focus for a minute on the joints which give you the possibility of motion. Different joints are capable of different actions. There are a few terms you should know in order to facilitate the discussion of joint actions.

Some joints allow only two actions. They either *flex* (bend) or *extend* (straighten). An example of this is the knee. Other joints, such as the hip joint, flex and extend too, but they have other actions as well. All of the appendages (legs, arms, head) can *rotate* at the point where they join the torso. A rotary action is one in which the body part holds its own place in space, but twists around itself. In other words, it rotates around its own axis. The arm can rotate in the shoulder joint, the leg in the hip joint, and the head on top of the spine.

Circumduction is an action that occurs when one end of a body part is fixed at its attachment and the other traces a circular path in space. An example of this action is a swing of the arm from the shoulder joint. The circle need not be complete.

LEARNING EXPERIENCE
By yourself, improvise with your concentration on the joints and their actions, rather than on the body parts which meet at these joints. Explore the range and type of each joint's movement. Allow your total body to participate but, through your skill, draw the attention to the selected joint you are exploring. Experiment with new placements of joints in space. Arrange a sequence of joint actions, projecting each new joint in its turn.

---

3. Motional experiences with body parts develop more sensitive articulation for the dance.

The *torso* is the center of your physical control. It is the trunk from which the movements of your limbs originate. The torso—spine, hips, shoulders, that which encloses the apparatus of the heart, lungs and the vital organs of life—is quite naturally the center of movement and feelings.

LEARNING EXPERIENCE

While sitting, lift up in your torso with a breath, stretch long in your lower back, and at the same time lift under your ribs and up through your sternum. Counterbalance this by pulling down in your shoulder blades and up through the back of your neck. Move away from this centered position and note the tendencies for movement of adjustment in the whole torso, as well as in your arms and legs.

The *upper torso* is an important area, as it affects breathing, the use of the arms and the uplifted appearance of the whole body. It is, however, one of the areas of least mobility because of the rib cage residing there. It is necessary to work conscientiously to accomplish the subtle articulations possible to this area.

LEARNING EXPERIENCES

Lift and carry your rib cage straight across to the right, through center, over to the left and through center again. Press it forward, come center, press out through your upper back, then return. (Keep your hips stationary, with the shoulders maintaining a horizontal line.) Circle the upper torso, carrying the rib cage from right to forward to left and back, around a vertical axis, in a horizontal plane.

Arch your body to the side by squeezing your right ribs together. Now arch to the same side by lifting your ribs, pressing up with your left side, leaving no wrinkles in your leotard. Check yourself in a mirror to see the different line, as well as the different feeling, of these two actions.

If the *head* is used as an extension of the action of the upper torso, the result is one of harmony in the body parts. If you carry your head rigidly, or in a direction opposite the body lean, you will feel a contrast of pulls and a sense of conflict. Be aware of the effects on the body and the feelings resulting from different uses of the head.

The *lower torso* is of equal and perhaps greater importance, for here is located your true center of gravity and the control for your legs, both in gesture and in weight-bearing functions. You should know what movement is possible in the lower torso, and how to control this area while others are moving so that balance is maintained.

LEARNING EXPERIENCES

With your shoulders and rib cage still, press from side to side through your hips. Press forward through your hip joints, then pull back through your lower back. Come to a centered position again. Holding all else still, circle your hips around a vertical axis, keeping your hip bones parallel to the floor.

Now, allowing your ribs and shoulders to participate, send your hips to the right and let your rib cage drop to the left. Again send your hips to the right, but this time lift your rib cage up and away from your right hip, arching up and over to the left. Feel the difference.

In a standing position, twist your hips to the left, resisting at first through your ribs, then letting your ribs follow, then your shoulder and even your arm. Then twist your hips back to the right, letting the rest of your torso follow sequentially.

There are a great many movements possible to the peripheral parts of the body: to the head, the arms and the legs. It is possible to move all these parts in isolation, or the motivation for the movement of the periphery can come from the center, making the statement with the total body. Either one is a legitimate use of the body, and each will probably find its place in your choreography.

The *arms* have many possibilities for action: lifting and lowering (forward and back and to the side), rotation and circumduction at the shoulder joint, not to mention the endless possibilities of variation when one adds actions of elbow and wrist joints. But it is not the "whats" that each joint can do, but "how" they can do them that make dance fascinating.

LEARNING EXPERIENCES

Start to lift your arms by pulling down on the muscles below your shoulder blades. Once your arms are at the horizontal, pull down even harder. Feel the deep connections of your arm muscles with your back.

Now lift your arms with as little torso participation as possible. Feel the difference between these two experiences.

Lift your right arm to the side, letting your hand begin the action. Now try the same action beginning with your elbow—and now with your shoulder. Finally, let your arm rise as a result of the sequential pressing to the side of your hip, rib cage and shoulder. Your arm rises as the result of the sideward unfolding of your whole body.

The arms have a natural tendency to reflect the movement of the rest of the body, and you will capitalize on this tendency much of the time. You may also find it of interest to try resisting this natural impulse.

LEARNING EXPERIENCE

Take a high lift in your torso up and over to the right, pulling your left arm down hard against it. Do the same action again, but continue the upward line of your spine with your arm. Note the difference in sensations.

Since there are two of them, your arms can become quite complicated in their patterns. They can move in unison with each other and with the torso, or opposite, not only to each other and to the torso, but to the legs and head.

LEARNING EXPERIENCE

Try lifting one arm forward while the other bends at your elbow joint across in front of your body. Meanwhile, twist your torso slightly to the left. Feel the result.

Hands can be one of the most magical and articulate parts of you. Sometimes this is to their detriment rather than their favor. There is so much movement possible for them that they often do things which distract from the real point of the movement, or which are inconsistent with its total quality. Imagine the little finger elegantly crooked, in the midst of strong angular motions of the arms and legs. This sometimes can happen without your slightest awareness. You should explore the possibilities for

movement in your hands, not only to know what is available for use, but also to develop an awareness of them and so make them consciously a part of your moving body.

LEARNING EXPERIENCES

Curl your fingers into your palm and open them out. As you curl your fingers, turn your palm down; as you open out, turn your palm up. With your open hand, spread your fingers wide apart and draw them back together; do this same thing with your arms extended forward at shoulder level, palms facing forward.

Now, to feel your fingers as extensions of your body, throw your right arm forward, allowing your fingers to open at the end of the throw. Feel the energy start from your shoulder and continue out through your fingertips. Find the right response for your hands in all other arm movements experienced so far.

Your *legs*, as well as your arms, lift and lower, rotate and circumduct. Their movement, however, differs from that of the arms in that their function is double. They are attached at the hip joint, so there is movement possible from there. They are also temporarily attached at the other end to the floor, responsible for supporting your weight or carrying it through space. There are times when their motional possibilities are more limited by this added responsibility than are the arms. Yet, the unique possibilities inherent in this limitation are quite fascinating.

While you are in this last position, consider that this "turned-
out" position of your hip joint is used a great deal in dance. This
is so for a number of good reasons. Among them is the fact that
the leg articulates more freely in the hip joint and bears weight
more securely in that position. Travel to the side is much more
easily done, and the sculptural lines of the body are often en-
hanced by the outward rotation of the legs.

The legs, even when not bearing weight, can still use their
contact with the floor to good advantage. In a leg swing, as the
leg brushes forward, the foot stays in contact with the floor until
its arc lifts it up into space. The energy that was first used to push
along the floor is then used to lift the leg. In a hop or jump, the
height of the elevation comes not only from the extension of the leg
joints, but also from the energy used in pressing away from the
floor. If the legs are used to make a quick gesture in the air, the
movement must of course be sharp, as the moment of suspension
is brief, but also very exciting.

It is fun to explore the potential movement of the legs when
they no longer bear your weight.

LEARNING EXPERIENCE

Lying on the floor, explore the combinations of flexion and extension of all your leg joints. Experiment with rotation and circumduction at your hip joint. Find new ways to support yourself while you discover new ways to use your legs.

Feet could be as articulate and mobile as hands. Unfortunately, they are usually used as solid blocks of support packed up tight in shoes. Consequently they lose a good deal of their flexibility and facility. Too often you consider them only as beasts of burden; however, as you sit and relieve them of their load, you may explore what they can do.

LEARNING EXPERIENCE

Curl and uncurl your toes; spread them apart; relax. Press down through your arches, then draw them up. Turn the soles of your feet toward each other, then away. Crawl up one leg with the toes of your other foot. Flex and extend your ankles in unison, then in sequence. Do different things with each foot at the same time. Explore all the possibilities, not only sitting, but lying down and standing.

The working of your legs is complicated by their double function of support and gesture. Much of their action is determined by the requirements of balance in a particular movement. Though they are attached to the hips and move by virtue of muscles originating there, they usually move independently of the hips. They move while the torso holds its stability. Lifting a leg will seldom be preceded by lifting a hip.

While awareness of each individual part of your body is important, even more important is your awareness of your *total body*, of the relationship of parts both at rest and in motion. Here, there is interaction and integration which can produce a symphony of movement, as well as a solo for one part.

LEARNING EXPERIENCE

Just as you improvised projecting awareness of single body parts, now improvise projecting your entire body. Make the viewer aware of your total body, rather than of any single part.

4. The parts of the body work together in a particular way for a particular effect.

So much for the separate parts of your body. As has been suggested throughout this section, the important thing is that all the parts are interconnected and interrelated. Movement of one part implies motional tendencies of the other parts. When the torso moves, for example, there seems to be a natural tendency for the arms, legs and head to accompany this motion in a particular way. If you wish to produce harmony, you allow these tendencies to be fully realized. If you wish to connote disharmony, you deny the natural complementary movement.

5. Physical laws affecting the body in motion determine limitations and potential for dance.

As well as being concerned with the action and force of your body, you should be interested in the forces of the world that act upon it. You must relate to and control these forces, and you must become aware of how these forces control and affect you. They are constant and continually operative, so your dealing with them is a must. You will use your body with or against these forces in overcoming inertia, resisting the pull of gravity, controlling momentum, using centripetal and centrifugal force, in order to control and execute balances, falls, turns and circles, to go easily from starts to stops to starts again and to change direction with clarity and control. These forces are present and real, and relating to them in a particular way has meaning inherent to it. You can choose to use them and relate to them in unorthodox ways. There are countless ways of going from a state of inertia into motion. You may dance in defiance of gravity, give in to it or build patterns of both in space.

5a. Gravity affects dance in balances, falls and elevations. You relate specifically to gravity in everything that you do. You hold your body up against the downward pull of it, in most cases. You rise above it in precarious balances, and give in to it in falls.

Consider the total body *holding up against* gravity—the standing alignment. In the standing position, you are making a statement of the verticality of the body. The length of the body is emphasized; therefore the spine is elongated and its curve minimized. The joints of the arms and legs are extended.

Your body has a *center of gravity*, a point at which all its weight is said to be concentrated. While this center of gravity actually lies somewhere in the middle of the pelvis, it is sometimes more convenient for the dancer to think of it as being in the sternum, since the placement of the chest is so important in balance. Therefore the body is in a balanced upright position when the sternum is centered over the base of support (foot or feet). In all balances, keeping the center of gravity over the base of support (ball of the foot) will stabilize the body. When you balance on one foot, you have a smaller base of support, so balance is more precarious than it is when standing on both feet.

The body will be able to hold its upright position with a minimum of effort if one part is placed directly on top of another —the head on top of the chest on top of the pelvis on top of the feet. If any parts are out of line, considerable muscular effort is needed to keep you upright. Let gravity work for you in this vertical alignment, so that you may direct your efforts toward moving the parts which should be moving, instead of merely standing up.

LEARNING EXPERIENCE

To find your best standing alignment, start with your feet parallel. Keeping your heels in the same place, rotate your legs out from your hip joint in one motion. Your toes now point out on an angle. Shift your weight forward slightly from your ankles, so that your weight is over the balls of your feet. You should be able to lift your heels off the floor and replace them with no visible forward or backward weight shift. There is no flexion at your knee or hip joints. Your spine is elongated from bottom to top, and its curves are somewhat flattened as a result of this lengthening. Your pelvis is level and vertical, with the tailbone neither tipped up in back nor tucked under in front. Your chest is lifted and your sternum is placed directly above the balls of your feet. Your ribs are flat, also relaxed. Your shoulders are dropped and relaxed, neither pressed forward nor pulled back. Your neck is long, with your head balanced easily on top of it.

To avoid confusion in thinking of the body as separate parts, pulling in here and pushing out there, it is suggested that you think of only two things when taking a standing position. One is the lengthening of the spine from the middle of the back, down through the tailbone and up through the top of the head. Then think of relaxing everything else not involved in this lengthening—the shoulders, the arms, the ribs, the buttocks and even the face. The result should be a feeling of lift, of compactness, of being "on top of yourself" without undue strain or tension.

Balance is something each person must discover for himself. When you achieve it, note the muscular feel at that moment, the relative placement of each part of the body, and remember it. Try to achieve that same alignment again and again until it becomes a habit.

Another law of physics relating to balance is the familiar one of *action and reaction*. For every action, there is an equal and opposite reaction. If, in your standing alignment, one part is out of the vertical line, there must be a compensatory shift out of line in the opposite direction by another part. If you lift a leg behind you, you must displace part of you in a forward direction in order to keep from falling—perhaps your chest or your arms— or you might shift your whole body slightly forward from the ankles.

LEARNING EXPERIENCES

Practice balancing on one foot. Place your chest over the ball of your foot and extend your ankle. If you fall forward, readjust. If you fall backward, compensate by moving your chest slightly forward. Find your own point of balance. Then consciously shift the position of your body and discover what sort of compensatory action is necessary for balance to be maintained. With one foot flat on the floor, work in different positions of your torso, twisting and bending, even to a position parallel with the floor. Find out how much movement is possible in this balanced position.

Improvise with another person, both of you working in positions of precarious balance, using each other for assistance. Realize the tremendous sensitivity and care necessary in maintaining this double balance.

Sometimes it is desirable to *give in to gravity*. Diving, dropping, falling and collapsing movements are important in the vocabulary of the dancer for changing levels of space and for the

quality of motion which results from the withdrawal of energy. As with other kinds of motion, you can participate in it with the total body or with a single body part. You might withdraw the energy from a raised arm in short successive drops, or you might choose to fall flat on the floor.

In falling, you will discover that a progression of parts rolling onto the floor in sequence will dissipate the force of the fall and save you from bruised knees and elbows. Counterbalance your weight as you go down, so that all the weight is not going into one part of the body near the floor, but so that some of it is held in the opposite, balancing part. You will learn, and hopefully not the hard way, that you should land on the padded parts of the body—not on the bony, jointed corners. From down, you will discover the way back up. Control the going down and up in the stronger areas of the body: the thighs, back and abdomen.

LEARNING EXPERIENCE
Explore the possibilities of falling, with various parts of your body starting down first—your hip, your knee, your shoulder, your head and your hand. Since you have to get up to explore the next way down, try different possibilities of rising from the floor.

A third way of using gravity is to *resist* it—to push away from the floor in hops, leaps and jumps. These adventures into open space are collectively called *elevations*. In order to elevate successfully, you must use more force in pushing yourself up than gravity uses in pulling you down. A good deep knee bend (*plié*) as preparation, followed by a swift extension of all the leg joints (*relevé*), will launch you. Applying the "action-reaction" principle again, the further down the knee bend takes you (within reason), the higher you should rise into the air.

Pliés and relevés, in addition to being important exercises for building leg strength, are the actions you do when taking off and landing from elevations. The plié is the preparatory flexion of the legs which gives you the power to rise, as well as the cushion which absorbs your weight as you land. The relevé is the forceful extension of the legs which sends you into the air, and the prelude to the landing plié which eases you back to the floor. The names for these actions are borrowed from French ballet, as are the movements themselves. But they are so integral a part of all dance that no one discipline can claim them as its exclusive property.

LEARNING EXPERIENCES

To practice the plié, begin with your body in good alignment and your legs turned out at your hip joint. As your legs bend, direct your knees out over your feet. For a demi-plié (small), flex your legs only until your heels want to lift from the floor. At this point, return to the starting position by straightening your knees, keeping them turned out all the while. For a grande plié (large), continue your knee bend down past the point where your heels lift from the floor to where your hips are just elevated from your heels and the weight still carried in your thighs. The return occurs by placing your heels down as your body lifts, and then extending your knees. In both pliés, your spine maintains its length and alignment and your pelvis tips neither forward nor back.

To practice the relevé, stand again in good alignment with your legs turned out at your hip joint, and slowly extend your hips, knees and ankles to their maximum, so that your body rises on the balls of your feet. Then, keeping your knees straight, lower your heels to the floor, opposing this downward action with a feeling of lifting through your chest at the same time.

You will no doubt practice pliés and relevés a great deal in the course of your class. They are highly important exercises in themselves, as well as vital to elevations. They build strength in the hips and legs, and provide continual opportunity to practice good alignment. They are the means by which the body changes level and travels upward and downward. So important are they that the dancer performs them repeatedly, almost like ritual prayer, in his daily training.

Once you are in the air in an elevation, you have no balance problem. As you require no support, you do not have to worry about it—that is, until you have to land. Before landing, prepare a base of support (a foot or feet), and see that your center of gravity is placed over it. The body may do all kinds of things once it is in the air, but it should be in proper alignment when taking off or it may be misdirected in the air.

LEARNING EXPERIENCE
Practice jumping in all directions, including turning. Jump with your legs in various relationships in the air. Jump with your body making different shapes in the air.

5b. Centrifugal and centripetal forces affect a body in circular motion. Another physical law which you will encounter when doing turns and circles is the one involving centrifugal and centripetal forces. You have experienced centrifugal force when, as a child, you stood in one spot and whirled around with your arms out wide and felt the tingling sensation of blood rushing to your hands. (This may be a good time to recall that feeling.) *Centrifugal force* is that which tends to impel a thing toward the outside of a center of rotation. This is counterbalanced by *centripetal force,* which pulls inward toward the center of rotation. You may have experienced this force as a child, too, when you rounded the corner on your bicycle and leaned inward to make the turn. If you leaned in too far, you fell off and became painfully aware of the dangers of unbalanced centripetal and centrifugal forces.

When you move through space in a curved path, you will find that these forces work upon you just as they do upon any circling body. You will find yourself molding your body to the shape of the curve, leaning inward with part of your body to counteract the outward force of the turn. The faster you go, the stronger the effect of these forces. It is the "hows" you discover to balance these forces which make turning and circling so interesting and exciting. There is always one more way to turn.

In *turning*, you revolve around an imaginary axis that runs vertically somewhere through your body. It may go from your head through a point between your feet, if you are upright and turning on both feet. Or, if you are doing a tilted turn on one foot, the theoretical axis may go through one shoulder down through the ball of the foot. You may even turn and travel through space at the same time, taking the imaginary axis with you. However you turn, it is the quality of the turn that you want to bring out in your performance. It is the continuity of the revolution which gives turning its character as a motion.

Circling, as opposed to turning, involves moving through space around an imaginary vertical axis which lies outside the body. More simply, it is moving on the outside edge of a circle. You will feel your relationship to that circle's imaginary center and discover what adjustments you must make to centrifugal and centripetal force to keep moving in that circular path. Again, it is the quality of the curve that is to be brought out in your performance.

You can also move in curved paths in a vertical plane. These vertical curves are often referred to as *overcurves* and *undercurves*. As their names imply, the overcurve describes the top half of a circle, and the undercurve describes the bottom half.

Overcurves and undercurves rely heavily on the use of the plié and relevé. An undercurve can begin in relevé, but usually begins in normal standing position. Try one.

LEARNING EXPERIENCE
With the weight on your right foot, plié, lowering the weight of your body. Transfer your weight forward in plié to your left leg, and straighten it. The undercurve has been accomplished.

You may perform an undercurve with the whole body or with one part. A leg swing is an undercurve. The on-the-ground phase of the skip is also an undercurve.

An overcurve usually begins in plié, particularly since it often involves air moments, for which a preparation for take-off and a cushioned landing are essential.

LEARNING EXPERIENCE

Your weight is on your right leg and the path of travel is up and forward. Straighten your leg to relevé. Transfer your weight forward to your left foot in relevé. Lower your weight by pliéing your left leg. Try it now with a push-off, so that an air moment occurs during the transfer of weight from one foot to the other.

An overcurve is the path the body follows in a leap, jump or any elevation that travels through space.

LEARNING EXPERIENCES

Improvise movements entirely in curved paths. Let all your gestures be rounded. Let your feet trace only curved paths on the floor, and let your body always shape to the arc of the movement.

Improvise with a group, wherein only one person is self-starting. The others can begin motion only when a moving body comes near them. The paths of motion are always orbital, or circular, and can change only when made to do so by the passing or colliding force of another body. Try to let your body react as a freely moving object in space, without imposing your will upon its motion.

5c. Inertia and momentum must be considered in designing "going" and "stopping" in dance. Finally, you will be concerned with overcoming *inertia*, with the gathering up of energy to move from a static position. This can take the form of a *gesture* in which one part of the body moves through space, or in the form of *locomotion* in which the whole body moves through space and across space. In either case, energy must be expended to make the initial move. Once the action is begun, its momentum will carry it along until the motivating energy runs out or until more energy is summoned to halt the momentum.

Gestures, such as arm swings, leg swings and head nods, are done in one place and need no extra consideration, unless done with such extreme force that the body is sent off balance or off through space. Sometimes this is done intentionally, with the rest of the body following sequentially, and still under control. At other times, it is as though this part of the body were possessed of another spirit. For the most part, gestures are isolated actions, with the torso holding upright or molding to be in consonance with the gesture. Gestures of two parts at once—such as leg and arm swings—are usually done in opposition to maintain balance.

In locomotion, however, there are several additional considerations. When the whole body begins to move through space, there must first be a weight shift in the direction of travel in order to overcome inertia. In order to take a step forward, for example, there is a shift of weight into a forward direction and then a receiving of it on a new base of support—the other foot. The timing of the weight shift and the placing of the new base is variable, but in normal walking they occur in sequence: the weight begins to shift forward, a new base is formed to receive it and the weight arrives over the new base of support.

Conversely, when one wants to stop, *momentum* must be overcome. The weight, which has been displaced in the direction travelled, must be brought back over the base of support.

LEARNING EXPERIENCE
Run at full speed and stop suddenly. Notice how your weight shifts backward before you stop. Now try to stop without this weight shift. Be careful.

Locomotion is usually defined as movement through space, carrying the weight from one base of support to another. As in the above, the bases of support are usually thought of as the feet, but there are many other possibilities. All the other parts of the body can be used in combination.

LEARNING EXPERIENCES
Explore ways of going through space on your back, on your side and on your stomach. Use your feet and hands for pulling and pushing. Try locomotion on anything but your feet.

Find locomotions involving transfer of your weight to different bases of support. You may use your feet as well as anything else that will hold you. Use four supports, then try two, then one. Vary these by changing your facing. Face the floor, the ceiling and then the wall as you travel.

The conventional and generally accepted basic methods of locomotion on foot are as follows:

1. *Walk*—the simplest kind of locomotion. A walk is a transfer of weight from one foot to the other.

2. *Run*—an extension of the walk. A run is also a transfer of weight from one foot to the other, but the stride is longer and the speed of travel faster. There is a brief moment in which neither foot is in contact with the floor.

3. *Leap*—a further extension of the run. A leap also goes from one foot to the other, but the distance covered is even greater than in the run, and the air moment longer.

4. *Hop*—a transfer of weight from one foot back to the same foot. The take-off and landing foot are the same, and there is necessarily a moment of elevation.

5. *Jump*—a landing on two feet after a take-off from one or both feet. The body is airborne at one moment during the jump.

There are also the following well known combinations:

6. *Skip*—a combination of a walk (or step) and hop.

7. *Gallop*—a combination of step and leap, moving forward.

8. *Slide*—a combination of step and leap, moving sideward.

LEARNING EXPERIENCES

Improvise on the simplest of these locomotions, the walk. Walk heel first, then toe first, turned in, turned out, and both fast and slow. Try many different uses of your feet and legs.

Devise a number of different movement combinations for yourself, about 8 to 12 counts in length, using the above means of locomotion. Practice them until you can do them with ease. Name the locomotions aloud as you do them, and have someone watch you to see if you are really doing what you say you are.

Both gesture and locomotion may be either straight or curved in their line of action. The arrival point may be the same, but the itinerary can be different. Take the gesture of reaching the hand forward to shoulder level. The hand starts hanging down by the side. It can travel up the body and forward to shoulder level by means of alternate flexion and extension of the shoulder and elbow joints, describing a path of two straight lines. It can also travel in a circular path, as in an arm swing, with a circumduction action at the shoulder joint.

Locomotion, as you have seen, can travel along a circular path in the horizontal or vertical plane. In the horizontal plane, the motion can curve either to the right or the left. In the vertical plane, the curve can be either under or over.

Locomotion in a straight path occurs in any of ten directions. They are: *forward, backward, sideward right, sideward left, forward diagonal right, forward diagonal left, backward diagonal right, backward diagonal left, up* and *down*. It sometimes aids our understanding of these directions to think of the body as the center from which forces arise and radiate in all directions. No matter which way the body faces, these directions are relative to the body itself (sideward right is always toward the dancer's right-hand side).

If all these forces are operating upon the body with equal strength, their effects balance each other out and the body remains in one place. In order to move in any direction, you must think of releasing the force pulling in the opposite direction. For instance, if you wish to go forward, you release the backward energy and give in to the forward one. Of course, these forces, with the exception of gravity (the downward one), are imaginary. But keeping their images in mind lends additional pungency and vitality to the quality of your movement through space. Moving into the backward direction becomes just that— totally and devotedly. It is *not* moving away from forward; instead, the forward force is released, and energy is dedicated to the motion backward.

LEARNING EXPERIENCES

Walk forward through space. Be sure that your total attention and total body are forward, with nothing left behind, straying out to the sides, pushing up or pressing down. Now walk backward in this same way, feeling your whole back press through space. Now go sideward, and feel the pressure of air along the whole side of your body.

Combine four steps forward, four steps sideward right, four steps backward and four steps sideward left in a square or box pattern. Now use the same arrangement of steps but change your facing in space, so that all your steps follow one straight line across the floor.

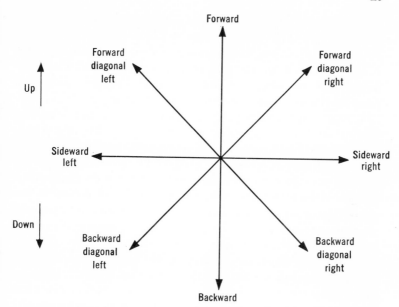

To summarize, in order for motion to occur, the weight must be shifted in the direction of the desired motion. To maintain balance, the weight must be directly above the base of support, counteracting the downward pull of gravity. This holds true for almost any locomotion which uses the feet as a base of support.

LEARNING EXPERIENCE

Practice walking, running and other locomotions with different placements of your chest. Try them with your chest over the base of support—then in front of it, then behind it. Note what compensations you have to make with other parts of the body to keep from falling. Notice the different rates of speed at which you can move with these various chest placements.

---

6. For dance, the fullest movement potential of the body should be developed.

In modern dance, there are really no right and wrong movements. There are those movements which are better for general use than others because they are more efficient, more harmonious to the body's structure and more pleasing to watch, but these usages are not absolute, and they can be deliberately distorted if that is the effect you wish to create.

One of your goals as a dancer is to be able to use your body in any way you decide, within its capabilities. You may have discovered from past experience that there are certain movements and controls which require skills you do not yet have. The greatest facility in movement requires the greatest range of motion in your joints, the greatest refinement of your movement-producing muscles, adequate strength in the muscles bearing greatest stress and a carefully developed sense of rhythm and balance. Which of these skills can be developed if you do not already possess them? By hard work and continual attention, all of these can be developed to a degree limited only by the structure of each individual body. Adequate body facility includes lengthening of the muscles of the back, backs of the legs and insides of the legs; it also includes strengthening of the muscles of the abdomen, back, thighs, calves, hips and feet. The necessary co-ordination and sense of rhythm is the result of practice involving all parts of the body working together, as well as the soloing of individual parts.

Books and teachers can provide exercises or techniques for developing these capacities. By shifting your mental focus, you can use these technical tools in many ways. You should always have a particular point of view about even the simplest exercise you do, so that you know what it is you want from that exercise and can focus your concentration on getting it. Even in the simple plié, you may focus on the totality of movement down and up, outward rotation of the thighs, length of the lower spine, lift of the sternum and balance of body parts in their verticality, the ease of the chest and arms, placement of weight on the soles of the feet, inner muscular sensations anywhere in the body, or any one of a number of other things. The possibilities are limitless; this is why the dancer can keep finding new mysteries, new delights and new benefits in his "ritual prayers" year after year. It takes a great deal of intelligent and sensitively aware hard work to attain a responsive and expressive body instrument, but many have felt that it was worth it. The rewards do not wait until the end, but happen daily in the delight of a balance held a few seconds longer, an intricate co-ordination mastered or the total fulfillment of a gesture.

However, the strengths and flexibilities resulting from these techniques may not be very meaningful to you unless you really need them in actualizing a movement pattern or dance idea. No one is really too impressed by your ability to put your ankle over your ear, and this has little to do with dance. Virtuoso technique is not an end in itself, but only a means to allow you to do whatever you want to do to the fullest extent. A skilled body is akin to a well-polished car with a well-tuned motor without a driver and with no place to go. When you are the one driving and when you have your own direction, then you will know what is required for the trip and will prepare ahead for it.

Concept III—Sensitive and Particular Selection and Shaping of the Abstract Elements of Dance Is What Determines It as Art

PREPARING THE BODY for dance is no more art than is a pianist's learning five-finger exercises. This is the craft—the mechanics which allow you to assemble the elements of your art skillfully. It is the elements of the art, rather than its craft, with which you will now be concerned.

Dance, and indeed all movement, happens in a space, uses up time and requires energy. These are the abstract elements of the art. In the following pages there are experiences which will acquaint you with the several facets of these elements, allow you to experiment with them in your own way and sharpen your artistic judgment in regard to their use in your dances.

Art starts when you begin to be concerned with other than the body instrument and the work done: when you are careful about and sensitive to the space you use, the time you take and the energy you exert in making shapes with your body and lines in space. When you are concerned not just with getting to the destination, but more with how you get there, you begin to dance.

The following pages include many experiences in the abstract elements of dance. Try them all. Try some of them more than once, changing the emphasis of the problem from one aspect to another.

1. The aspects of space must be studied and explored for clear and meaningful movement.

The space you have to work *in* as a dancer is, simply, all the space that happens to surround you on the stage, in the studio, in the gymnasium or wherever your work area may be. The space you have to work *with* is a different matter. This space is extremely flexible. In fact, you can make it appear or disappear at will, through your skill in creating illusions. Through different emphases, you can make your audience actually see what they might otherwise regard as empty space. You can create objects in space, within the viewers' imaginations and yours, and destroy them just as readily. You can even make spaces within spaces.

1a. Shape is the three-dimensional space concern of the total body. Shape is one of the strongest visual components of dance. It is present in every moment of every motion, and it is one of the things that the viewer's eye retains longest after the performance is over. Shape is the sculptural design of a body, a group of bodies or bodies and their prop or costume extensions. The spatial relationships of the bodies or of their component parts create the sculptural shapes.

Shapes are lines and angles, chunks and masses. While you are concerned with the look of these shapes from the outside, you will be concerned also with the kinesthetic feeling of these shapes.

Your body, by virtue of having a number of long, straight bones, is naturally facile at making shapes with straight lines and angles.

LEARNING EXPERIENCE

Using the mirror if you wish, design at least ten straight-line shapes for your body. Sense the muscular feel of each shape and check the mirror for the visual impact it might make on an audience. Now design ten more straight shapes without the use of the mirror, sensing only through your body how the shapes must look from the outside.

Softer, curved shapes are also possible. You already have a series of natural curves in your spine, and even the angular arms and legs can, by illusion, be formed into curves by using only a slight degree of flexion.

LEARNING EXPERIENCE

Repeat the above experience, using curved shapes. To begin with, start the curve in the center of your torso, using your deep central muscles to produce it. Then let the curve find its way out into the periphery.

Explore as many shape variations as possible with your own body. You can make slim or wide shapes, harmonious or dissonant shapes, solid shapes or shapes with holes in them. Try to relate different body parts in unusual ways—a knee to an earlobe, an elbow to a hip bone.

LEARNING EXPERIENCE
Make at least 25 of the most diverse shapes with your body. Be aware of the kinesthetic feel of each shape.

Do not preplan your shapes. The most exciting moments often occur when you act first and think about it afterwards. The body has a way of taking over, if you let it, and the spontaneous things that happen are often far more interesting than anything you could plan intellectually. In fact, accidents are the way almost all original things are created, because the mind tends to think first of things already experienced.

LEARNING EXPERIENCE
Improvise on the idea of shape. Spend your time between shapes not planning the next one, but sensing how it feels to be in the present one. Shorten the time interval between shapes, until you are doing a new shape every second or two. Do not give yourself time to preplan them.

When you dance alone, it is easy for an audience to see your shape, as it is outlined by the space surrounding it. Your intrusion into bare space breaks that space up into smaller pieces, which themselves are shapes. Try standing with your legs in a wide sideward stride. Now you have created a triangular space, bounded by your two legs and the floor. You yourself have a shape, and that space which you have created also has a shape. In art, this is sometimes referred to as *negative space*. Change the shape of that space between your legs and the floor.

As you work with more and more people, the resulting shapes become increasingly complex. We see the shape of a single tree in a meadow by the shape of the space around it and the negative spaces between the leaves and branches. What makes a tree difficult to see in a forest is the lack of surrounding negative space. As you work with a partner, and finally with a group, be sensitive to the negative spaces created by your positive body shapes.

LEARNING EXPERIENCES

Work in pairs. Partner A makes a shape for his own body. Partner B relates to that shape by fitting himself into one or more of the negative spaces created by A's shape. Partner B holds his shape, while A pulls out of his original shape and fits himself into the negative spaces created by B. Both will leave some negative spaces free, so that the resulting combined shape can be clearly seen.

Try this experience with three or more dancers. Remember that as more people are added, the total shape will become more complicated, and therefore each individual shape should be kept simple. Keep enough negative spaces in the design so that it makes a coherent whole, rather than a miscellaneous tangle of arms and legs (unless you want a comedy).

Stationary shapes are fine, but rarely do you dance standing still. Finding a way to move through space and still retain the character of your shape can be fun. You might be able to locomote on two feet, or you might have to travel on other bases of support.

LEARNING EXPERIENCES

Improvise with shape, moving across the floor. Design a shape before starting, and see how you can travel through space and still hold the shape you have made. Try some shapes on a two-foot base. Try some shapes that rest on other parts of your body besides your feet. How can these shapes travel?

Try the preceding experience with a partner. See what adjustments are caused by your spatial dependence upon one another as you try to locomote in your combined shape.

In order for dance to occur, shapes must change. Movement occurs in going from one to the next. Though no formula can be set down for finding the best way for a shape to begin to move, by and large the motion which seems the most natural is a good one to choose. Another possibility is a motion that begins from the

focal point of the shape itself. For instance, consider the shape of the body in its normal standing position, but with the head tilted to one side. The focal point of this shape is obviously the strange placement of the head and the neck. Because they are at odds with the rest of the shape, and with the body as you are accustomed to seeing it, your attention is immediately drawn to that area. It would seem logical, then, that the first movement of that shape might start somewhere in the neck, rather than in an arbitrary place like a foot or hand. One clue to finding the focal point of a shape, though not always accurate, is to find the place of strongest kinesthetic feeling in the body. In the shape just described, the muscular sensation in the neck is quite strong, fairly shouting that this is the place where motion should begin.

LEARNING EXPERIENCES

Start in the shape shown in the first photograph on this page, and find where to go from there. Listen to your body. Hold the position long enough to know where the focal point of the shape lies, then continue from there. Go from there into the next logical shape, experiencing each progressive change and knowing how other shapes should continue. Try the same procedure with the next two photographs.

Make at least 15 body shapes of your own and devise their first movements. Discover where the movements should start and what those movements should be. Repeat the experience, in dual shapes, with a partner. Try to sense, without verbal communication, where the first motion of your combined shape would begin.

The dancer in motion is like a moving picture. If you stopped the film, or the dancer, at any given moment, there would be a frozen shape in the arrested motion. Although the dancer may be aware of the more obvious shapes he makes, he must also be aware of the continuously changing shapes he makes en route—that is, in transition from one shape to another.

LEARNING EXPERIENCES

Design two different shapes. Then devise a way of getting from the first to the second, starting the motion at its most logical place in your body and proceeding as directly as possible to the second shape.

Design a series of ten shapes. Choreograph the transitions between these shapes.

Shape, then, is one aspect of space that is always present in dance—as you can see in the stop-action of a film. The dancer may emphasize or de-emphasize shape, depending on his purpose, but he should be aware of its presence in all motion.

1b. The body in motion can carve a shaped volume of space out of the surrounding area. *Volume* is an aspect of space that is somewhat related to shape, but it concerns itself primarily with negative or surrounding space, rather than with the positive space of the dancer's body. Because volume is created out of negative space, it is up to the dancer to establish the dimensions of that volume for the audience and to make them see it as if it actually existed.

Volume can be said to be a piece of space encompassed by boundaries. A volume can exist anywhere in the space through which a dancer moves. The dancer defines the boundaries, either partially or wholly, by using his body, and therefore defines the volume.

As an example, consider the shape of your arms as they form a circle in front of your chest, parallel to the floor. They create the partial boundaries of a volume of space. The volume might be spherical, as if you were holding a beachball, or it might be cylindrical, as if you were enclosing a tall column. You could further define the exact shape of that volume through motion.

Now bring your arms out to shoulder level. There are several possibilities here. You might deal with the volume of space between your arms and the floor. You could compress or expand that volume. You could lift or lower the volume of space above your arms, or even carry it through space with you. Through your imaginative use of movement, you can create, change or even destroy any volume you wish in the space around you.

LEARNING EXPERIENCE
Improvise with six different arm placements. Consider them the partial boundaries of a volume of space. See how many different volumes you can create with each position. Do the same with the volume created by six different leg arrangements.

Volumes of space can be created between any parts of your body. Do not be confined to arms and legs. You can create volumes between your legs and chest, between your arm and your side or between your head and the floor. You need not describe the total boundary of the volume. Often a partial indication will be enough to establish its size.

LEARNING EXPERIENCES
Improvise with volume as your main idea. Create volumes in space. Change the size of these volumes.
With a partner, experiment with creating volumes between the two of you. Change the size, shape and location of the volumes. Expand them; compress them.

Sometimes you may wish to establish a volume in space, go away from it and then return to it. If your definition of the volume is sufficiently strong, you can make the audience see that volume as still existing where you put it, even if you leave it for a while.

LEARNING EXPERIENCES

Work with an actual object—a box, a table, a bench or other simple prop. Define its volume. You may want to trace its outline with your hands, for example, or its height by sitting on it. Be very clear in your definition. Now remove the actual object and establish the same volume in space. Be just as clear in defining its boundaries.

Work in a group. Have several objects scattered in the working space. They should be objects which can be moved on, under or through. Establish the shape of each object in space. Now remove the actual objects and restate their volumes in space. Move among them as if they still occupied their former spaces—in other words, be careful not to walk through a table.

Again, work in a group. Establish a volume in space, perhaps a simple geometric figure. Through movement, indicate its boundaries. You may work outside or inside the volume. Now move it from place to place. Change its position in space, but do not destroy the form.

1c. The dimension of a movement must be carefully defined for clarity of meaning. *Dimension* in dance is the definition of the space in which one works—its *height*, its *width* and its *depth*. The depth dimension includes the directions of forward and backward; the width dimension includes the sideward directions, while the height dimension deals with the directions of up and down.

Your specific use of space can produce varied effects. Limiting movement to a sideward dimension might be one way to qualify the space around you. By setting up limits such as this when dealing with a movement problem, you will often find the most exciting solutions.

LEARNING EXPERIENCES

Limit yourself to the exploration of a two-dimensional space—forward and backward, side to side, diagonally or up and down. Keep your body thin and narrow, and the motion as nearly as possible in a two-dimensional plane. Improvise.

Working with a partner, improvise in the same two-dimensional plane. (The addition of another person can amplify dimensional experiences.)

Again, work with a partner, each in a two-dimensional space, but this time in contrasting dimensions—depth against width or diagonal against height.

One aspect of the height dimension is level. In modern dance, you can work in any level of the space which you can reach, from prone on the floor to the greatest height you can jump. With the aid of prop extensions, you might reach even higher. For the most part, though, when you move on your feet you move in one of three levels—low, middle and high. Of course, there is nothing in your improvisations which limits you to moving only on your feet.

LEARNING EXPERIENCE

Singly, in partners or in a group, explore the space parallel to the floor at different levels. Sense the movement at each plane, the parallel relationship to the floor and the relative distances from the floor to the various levels.

Another aspect of dimension is distance. When you decide to move into a forward direction, you must immediately make another decision—how far? An inch? A foot? As far away as you can reach? Farther than you can reach? There is enormous room for variation in the size of a movement, from a purely physical standpoint. You can make a forward gesture of the hand that involves the most minute movement of the wrist, or you can make one for which the whole body must wind up to project that hand forward into space.

LEARNING EXPERIENCE

Explore the possibilities of various sizes of movements. Find large movements for small parts of your body and small movements for large parts. Using one body part, begin with small motion, progress to larger motion and back down to small—both gradually and suddenly. Make large movements in one body part and small movements in another at the same time. Move with or against another person in large and small relationships.

Beyond the physical limits of the body, you have additional means to achieve enormous distance. By projecting the psyche into space at the same time, you can create the illusion of limitless distance. The totality of the co-ordination between the psyche and the body is primarily responsible for the phenomenon of *projection*. Spatial projection is but one facet of total performing projection.

LEARNING EXPERIENCE

Choreograph a short phrase. Treat the space around you in three different ways as you perform the phrase. Emphasize the space: 1) one foot away from you, 2) as far as you can reach, 3) to infinity.

1d. The floor pattern of a dance influences its aesthetic effect. As you move through space during a dance, you trace a pattern through that space; this is sometimes called the *floor pattern*. If you had wet paint on your feet, this floor pattern would be obvious at a single glance. The audience sees this floor pattern not at one glance, but gradually—in time—as you make it. Floor patterns can be more or less important, depending on the dance. You should be aware of their existence, so that you may use them to advantage and avoid their pitfalls. Keep your floor patterns interesting. Unless it is your particular aim to impress your audience with monotony, do not choreograph a whole dance in circles.

LEARNING EXPERIENCE

Devise for yourself, by moving or drawing, a floor pattern of walks that goes in most of the eight horizontal directions (see page 28). Include some curved paths, if you wish, either horizontal or vertical ones. Then, using the same floor pattern, choreograph more interesting locomotor movements to substitute for the walks. Finally, choreograph the rest of your body's movements to complement the locomotor movements you have devised. Perform the three separate facets of this experience. Try to retain the clarity of your original floor pattern, even though the movement on top of it has become more complex.

The floor pattern can determine the motional line of a body. A strong run in a straight diagonal path requires almost a straight forward diagonal lean of the body. On the other hand, the floor pattern can be an outgrowth of the shape or motional line of the body. If a movement begins in the curving of the torso and zig-zagging of the arms, a later development of this pattern may carry out the use of the original curve and zig-zag in its floor pattern.

LEARNING EXPERIENCE

Choose a shape, perhaps a good one from your recent experiences in shape. Retain it long enough to realize the linear implications within it. Then develop a locomotor pattern from this shape, using the lines of that shape as a pattern for your floor design.

The space around you, as you know, is not really empty. It is full of molecules, as is everything made of matter. The higher the concentration of molecules, the denser the matter. The air in the space around you is not very dense; you find it relatively easy to move through it. Yet, through your performing skill, you can create the illusion of density of space. Use your past experiences and your imagination to help you. Almost all people have had the experience of trying to walk through water. What were some of the physical changes in your movement which were caused by the density of the water? How might you move if there were no resistance at all to your motion?

LEARNING EXPERIENCES

Improvise with at least three different densities of space. Establish each density in a given section of your working space. As you move from "thick" to "medium" to "thin," let your motion reflect the changing density of the surrounding space.

Finally, having experienced space in all these various ways, choreograph a short study in which space is your main focus. Project this element to your viewers, above and beyond all others. Make them aware of space, rather than of motion, energy, time or you.

---

2. Time is an organizing factor in movement and in choreography.

Dance, as well as every other activity in this world, occurs in *time*. Again, the time you have to work *in* is all the time you have to give to your work. The time you have to work *with* is immediate or infinite, but it will be a piece of time carved out for your particular purpose. A dance has a beginning, and 30 seconds later, or three minutes later, or an hour later, it has an end. What goes on in the dance within that time span may be slow or fast. It will be sensed as slow or fast by the motion of the body within that one piece of time. If the piece lasts for three minutes and you fill it with ten movements, slowness will probably be sensed. If you fill it with 300 movements, fastness will be the result. Two aspects of time with which you will be concerned next are *duration* and *speed*.

As you become more and more sensitive to your own motion, you become aware of how long each motion lasts. It may be a fraction of a second, or it may be a full minute or even longer. The quality of motion is affected very definitely by its duration. Swing your arms in a full circle in one second. Make the same motion again, but take one minute to complete it. Walk around the room, taking two steps every second. Then try taking five seconds for each step, and then ten seconds for each step.

No doubt the muscular feel of the motions of short duration were much different from the feel of those which took a long time. You may have recognized totally different qualities, even though the motions themselves were essentially the same, except for their time values.

LEARNING EXPERIENCE
Select four or five different actions which are simple to perform, such as rolling, walking, standing up and sitting down, or scratching and stopping. Perform any of these actions at any time you wish, and for as long as you wish. Sense the duration of each action, and experiment with extremes of long and short duration. Be just as sensitive to the duration of the stops as you are to the actions.

To be able to sense how long a movement should continue is a valuable skill for a dancer. To sense how long a coffee break, a visit or a friendship should go on is a valuable skill for anyone. Sensitizing yourself to duration in movement should make you more aware of the whole pace of your life.

In many dances, metered music tells you exactly how long a

movement should be—half a beat, two beats or six beats. But it is likely that there will be times when there is no metrical beat to help you. Some modern choreographers create with a stop watch instead of a musical score. They determine that certain movements or phrases should last a given amount of time. Through repeated rehearsals, the dancers learn to judge these lengths of time with amazing accuracy. Music, or sound, is then composed in equivalent time units for the dance.

LEARNING EXPERIENCES

Work with a partner. Set an arbitrary duration, such as 20 seconds. Keep moving for what you believe to be 20 seconds, then stop. Your partner, armed with a stop watch or a watch with a second hand, will let you know how close you came to hitting the mark. Practice with a number of different durations.

Perform a movement combination that moves across the floor. Practice doing it with one or two other people, using no beat or accompaniment of any kind. Learn to sense between you the common duration of each movement, so that ultimately you are all moving simultaneously.

A sense of duration is particularly helpful to you in improvisation. Movement themes which are started in an improvisation need a certain amount of time to establish themselves. If this time is allowed to drag on too long, boredom sets in. If it is not long enough, a feeling of frustration and unfulfillment results. Try to be aware of this in your next improvisation. Try to find the "right" time to start a fresh action.

2a. Speed determines its own use of energy and the feeling of movement. Speed, of course, is the fastness or slowness of a motion. The range between faster-than-fast and slower-than-slow can be very great. Your ability to perform these extremes of speed may be greater than you think.

LEARNING EXPERIENCE

Perform several single movements as fast as you possibly can—so fast that the eye can barely follow them. Now try a movement as slowly as you can make it. See if you can move so slowly as to be almost imperceptible, like the minute hand of a clock.

Of course, you will not want to move slower-than-slow or faster-than-fast in every dance, but these tempos should be available to you when you want them. You will usually use a variety of speeds, some of them extreme. Nothing kills interest quicker than moderation. A good brisk accent in a series of slow movements, or a sudden sustained movement in the midst of a driving tempo can do wonders to enliven the audience, the dancer or the vitality of the movement itself.

LEARNING EXPERIENCE

Improvise freely by yourself, simply being aware of the speed of your motion. Try abrupt changes from slow to fast. Try gradual acceleration. Try coming out of a very fast movement immediately into a very slow one.

Speed and duration are, of course, interrelated. A fast movement has a short duration. A single movement of long duration will understandably be slow. Sometimes movements are repetitious, though, and a series of fast movements can last for a long time.

Single actions join other single actions into longer units known as *phrases.* A phrase may be of any duration and any speed, or several speeds. A phrase may consist of any number of separate motions, but its distinguishing feature is that it has a sense of semicompletion about it. Longer and longer time units occur as a dance progresses—phrases join to become a *section;* sections may join to become separate *acts* of an evening-length ballet; and finally, all the time units join to make a whole dance. A dance may be no more than a minute or no less than a full evening in length. Its duration will be determined by its content. When it feels completed, it is done; it lasts as long as it *should* last.

Highly organized time with an easily identifiable *beat* has become the custom in most music. You can probably hear organization in units of 2, 3 or 4, perhaps even in units of 5 or 7. Using this kind of *metered time* in dance, it is easy to tell the duration of a movement by counting the number of beats it occupies. A motion may take two beats, or counts, or it may take five and a half. Once the rate of speed of the beat is established, one has only to count off as many beats as are needed to know how long each particular movement lasts. Metered time is a convenient way to mark off time, particularly for a group of dancers; everyone is moving to the same time standard, so keeping together is no problem.

You can alter time as you alter space, by a particular use of movement. You can divide it into equal units and repeated rhythms, or into unequal units and different rhythms. It can appear to flow on, to stop altogether or to be broken up into chunks. A particular use of time will alter your movement. Tensions are created by gradually accelerating the speed of motion or by gradually shortening the units of division.

Every movement will have its own characteristic rhythmic structure. If you are tuned in to it, you can almost count out in consistent organization the rhythm of brushing your teeth or starting your car. Each activity has its own rhythm; even each feeling has its own rhythm because of the way it affects the heart and breathing apparatus.

LEARNING EXPERIENCES

Take an everyday activity and repeat it until you can do it without thinking about it, doing it consistently the same way every time. Now have someone clap a pattern of accents for you. Using this rhythmic pattern, find a new movement combination for it.

Build a rhythmic pattern, or use this one:

and find a movement pattern to fit it. Repeat the movement pattern enough times to sense the kinesthetic feeling which accompanies the rhythm.

Even though you will find that each motion falls into its own natural rhythmic pattern, it does not mean that you must be true to that pattern all the time. In dance, it is your privilege to alter movement characteristics. Doing familiar movements in erratic time patterns may result in a fascinating dance.

When you work with metered time, you will base your organization on an underlying pulse—a steady, even beat which is continuous. These beats can be separated into different group lengths by capitalizing the first beat in each group with an accent and by putting periods at the end of each phrase. Just as the words on this page are punctuated with commas, periods and semicolons, movement may be punctuated with changes of direction, sudden jumps or force accents. Phrases may begin with a bang and end logically with a period, or they may begin slowly and end suddenly in an exclamation point!

When you work with music, you will be aware of its organization into units. These units are punctuated by accents. Emphasis on the first of every three beats gives us ¾ time; emphasis on the first of every five beats gives us ⅝ time. In other words, your underlying beat is divided into measures each with a certain number of beats of equal duration.

LEARNING EXPERIENCE

Using a walk or run, move in ¾ time, accenting the first of each three beats by stamping, clapping or taking lower, longer or higher steps. Change direction on the first beat; jump on it. Do the same with ⅝ time. Notice the difference in feeling. Try the same thing with 4/4 time, and compare the feeling of this with the others. Now put together combinations of fives, fours and threes in ascending or descending order, or mixed.

Sometimes metered time is simply undesirable for a dance or an improvisation. Time can then be loosely structured or timed in seconds. In this case, the dancer's intuition is relied upon to judge how fast and how long he moves. When working with a group, it takes practice and sensitivity for all to establish a common time denominator without relying on a metrical beat. Such loosely structured time often allows for greater spontaneity between the dancer and the movement than does more organized, metered time.

LEARNING EXPERIENCES

Improvise freely to a metrical drum beat or to a piece of music. Move with the regularity of the beat. Now try to move against it. Alternate phrases that are "in time" with phrases that are "out of time."

Improvise with no beat at all on the subject of "move and stop." Be particularly sensitive to the speed with which you move, to the dura-

tion of your movement, to the silence you hear and to the length of the times when you hold still.

Work with a partner or in threes, having conversations in rhythms. Let one person start and the next react. Keep the rhythmic responses going as you would a verbal conversation. Clap, stamp or move your conversations. Make voice sounds.

Finally, draw upon the time experiences you have just had and choreograph a short study in which you present "time." Make your viewers see time *over and above all other aspects of motion.*

---

3. The amount of energy and method of its expenditure in dance may be determined by the time-space factors or by a particular motivation.

Energy is closely related to time and space. Slow movement in a small space takes little energy. Moving through a large space in a small amount of time takes lots of energy.

All motion requires energy. Even lying still, just breathing, takes some small effort to keep the diaphragm moving up and down. Energy is merely one of the factors which give a movement its particular quality.

Two types of energy are of concern to you in your study of dance. One is the obvious, *physical* energy needed to move muscle and bone. The other is *psychic* energy. There is nothing occult about this psychic energy. It is simply that which lends spirit and vitality to a dancer's motion through means other than physical.

Energy to move one's body is supplied by the contraction of the muscles. The greater the muscular job, the more energy that is required. To lift the entire weight of the body off the floor in a jump takes a great burst of energy. To raise one arm slowly takes very little. Each motion has its own minimum requirement of energy to accomplish that motion. Any more energy than that minimum makes the performance of the motion inefficient. This inefficiency can occur under two circumstances. One is that the dancer may have planned it that way to produce a particular quality of motion. The other is that he may not have discovered the proper amount of energy for movement and is using more than necessary, resulting in excess tension. This should be avoided, as tension will not only make the motion difficult to perform, but will also call attention to itself. The audience will then see the dancer's problems with the movement, rather than the quality of the motion being performed. The only valid reason for executing a movement with more tension than necessary is to alter the quality of the movement.

LEARNING EXPERIENCES

Extend one arm in front of you. Gradually increase the tension in that arm, without moving it, until it is as tense as you can make it. Notice the difference in the appearance of the arm itself. Release the tension quickly. Note the change.

Raise one arm from its normal position sideward to shoulder level. As you do, gradually increase the tension from none at all to very strong. Repeat the same action, starting with a maximum of tension, or energy, in the arm, and as the arm is raised, decreasing it to just enough energy to raise the arm. Perform the entire motion with a minimum of energy, then with a maximum of energy. Watch to see what quality changes occur as a result of the differences in energy.

Explore the sensation of tension. Allow it to build and then release in different parts of the body, and in the total body. In a state of great tension, try a movement pattern you have already done. Notice the change in feeling and its effects on the shape of your body and your breathing.

Finding the proper amount of energy to perform an action efficiently is a skill that has to do with the mechanics of dance. In the art of dance, you will employ your artistic judgment and make choices about how you are going to use energy, not just to perform a motion, but to produce a special quality of motion which you wish to project.

No one can tell you that a certain amount of energy or a certain way of expending it will give you the quality of motion you desire. You have to experiment to find this out for yourself, and others can only suggest what possibilities there may be.

You have a choice of the quantity of energy to use—a lot, a little or something in between. Of course, you know that the gradations between a lot and a little are many. Then you must choose the way you will spend this energy. Should you attack the movement explosively and let the energy gradually dissipate itself? Should you start gently and gradually build to great strength? Or should the amount of energy you use be the same throughout the movement or the phrase?

Your manner of releasing the energy you have collected for the movement is also a matter of your aesthetic choice. You may yield to gravity once in a while, in a swing, using only a little energy to pick up the upward tail of the swing. You might sustain a movement, so that no part of it is more or less forceful than another. You can let it out like sand pouring out of a sock, leaving you hollow and empty, or keep it within like a huge secret, giving out only an occasional glimpse of its potential. You might bounce, rebound, vibrate, collapse, shake or hurl yourself into space. The possibilities are limitless.

LEARNING EXPERIENCES

Improvise on any three of the energy possibilities mentioned in the preceding paragraph. Stay with each one long enough to explore in some depth its potentials for movement. Then intersperse the qualities as you improvise further. Be constantly sensitive to energy.

Compose a short study in which you project energy over all the other elements discussed.

Psychic energy is that intangible commodity which, it is said, gives life to your dancing. Like life, it is almost impossible to define. It might be defined as a spirit of vitality within you, a strongly-felt motivation to do and to move, an enthusiasm of the will, a projection of your mental self beyond your physical self. It is a state of being immediately present—of being mentally with your physical self in time, and not an instant behind or ahead of it. However it is defined, its presence or absence is immediately discernible in your ability to project movement. This magic of projection presents itself as a light in your eye, an extra millimeter of lift in your sternum, a feeling of totality and fulfillment of a motion, an illusion made credible.

The psyche is even more mobile than your physical self. You can withdraw it inside you, or project it out into infinity. It can ride on the surface of your skin, or shoot out through the top of your head. Take the trouble to find yours. No one can tell you how, but you might begin by looking inside yourself—by practicing internal awareness and sensitivity to the world around you, and to that "electricity" which connects you to all living things.

The elements of time, space and energy cannot be separated except for discussion. You do not make a single movement without using each one, and all simultaneously. The awareness of all these elements and their effect on each other make you aware of the possibilities of your art. You move with quality—the result of the sensitive use of time, space and energy in totally realized motion.

Concept IV—Improvisation Is an Indispensable and Exciting Part of the Dance Experience

IMPROVISATION—CREATING ON the spur of the moment—is an essential part of every creative art. The novel does not leap full-blown from the head of the writer onto the paper. He improvises words, sentences and outlines in his head before writing them down. The artist makes preliminary sketches before he paints. The musician experiments with combinations of sounds. For the dancer, movement improvisation is a prelude to choreography. It is also a tool for developing his performing sensitivity and a means of discovering his body's natural movement style, and it has potentiality as an art in its own right.

1. It is necessary to experience both structured and free improvisation.

Improvisation can be of two kinds—*structured* or completely *free*. In free improvisation, no subject matter is decided upon beforehand, no boundaries set or no limits imposed. You simply turn yourself on and begin to move, letting the improvisation progress continuously in any direction that may suggest itself as you go along. Your spontaneous response to previous material or your own present state of being and awareness directs the course of the improvisation. With free improvisation, you are likely to touch upon a broad spectrum of movement subjects, but there is a danger inherent in this way of working. With an unlimited subject, it is tempting to skim over the surface, doing the most obvious movements or the ones which come most naturally to your particular movement style. This is especially likely to happen at the beginning of the improvisation. You must persist for long enough to get out of this stylistic groove. Your body will ultimately become bored with the same old things; it is only then that fresh, new things will begin to happen.

1a. For the beginner, a limited improvisational situation is easier to handle. A second kind of improvisation is more highly structured. Until you are well practiced in the skills of improvisation, it will be wisest for you to work within limitations. These will be set ahead of time with reference to the subject matter of the improvisation. During improvisation, you respond not only to previous movement material, but continually in reference to the original problem. Keeping your improvisation related to the original problem will allow you to experience one thing in great depth, while in free improvisation, you may only skim the surface of a lot of things in serial order. It is in experiencing something in depth that you go beyond the most obvious, ordinary, comfortable movements and extend the range of your possibilities. You may use the problems suggested in this book or by your instructor, or you may originate your own. Devising your own is probably most desirable, because ultimately this is the way the mature artist works.

An improvisation almost has a life of its own. If you are open and allow the situation to take over, rather than try to force it in a direction you want it to go, you will be much more likely to have a new experience. After all, you grow only through new experiences and your reactions to these experiences. An improvisation is a situation which allows you to have a new experience, and the limits of the problem are the framework in which the experience can occur.

2. Improvisation serves many personal and dance needs.

Improvisation is a major part of your dance training and a valuable experience for anyone. Its purposes are many. For some of you, it may be the first creative experience you have had since childhood. Ask yourself how long it has been since you have relied completely on your imagination. You used to spend hours playing house, scribbling on blank pieces of paper or humming little tunes which you made up as you went along. As you grew older, you played games with prescribed rules, followed coloring book lines which someone else had drawn or sang songs which you learned in school. As an adult, your participation in art probably consists of reading, going to plays, concerts and galleries, or perhaps playing an instrument—but playing music written by someone else. What has happened to your own imagination along the way? Where is the spontaneity with which you used to get up a game of cops and robbers?

In improvisation, you are once again dependent on your own resources to tell you what to do. You have a chance to dust off that imagination and see if it still works. After a little practice, you will probably be surprised at how well it works. Whether or not you dance a step after this course is finished, this opportunity to take that aspect of your mind out of mothballs may be one of the most valuable experiences you will ever have.

But since we are considering you a dancer, at least for the duration of this class, let us see how improvisation serves you specifically in dance.

Knowledge of yourself is one of the more important functions of improvisation. You possess a unique body, so you cannot successfully take someone else's movement style and impose it on your own body. Through improvisation you experiment with your own instrument, exploring the limits of its capacity and discovering its natural style. Equally important, you explore the depths of your own imagination.

Choreography seldom takes place without being preceded by a great deal of improvisation, searching for movement materials. This is the "trial and error" method of the artist, and a good 90% of the improvised material is ultimately thrown out. The small percentage which is kept represents the choreographer's selection of his best material. Improvisation may give you ideas for new dances or indicate ways of progressing within a dance. Rarely is a successful dance composed cerebrally, without improvisation. The body has a way of finding fresh, pertinent things of which the intellect would never have thought. The more you improvise before choreographing, the greater your chance of originality.

2a. Improvisation is an agent of movement sensitivity. One of the important results of improvisation is the development of your sensitivity—sensitivity to time, to space, to energy, to yourself, to other people and to motion. This sensitivity is possible only when you concentrate fully on the present moment of the improvisation—a state of being totally "in" it. "In" is not a state of being lost in the improvisation beyond all awareness of outside considerations, but a state in which all these things are less important than the improvisation. When you are "in" it, you are no longer concerned with how you look, what is coming next, whether you will lose your balance or whether your toe is pointed or not. You are totally dedicated to the improvisation and to your sensing of it. When you are not "in," you appear to be mentally on the outskirts of the improvisation. It is as if your mind were once removed from the proceedings, even though your body may be there. You are not "in" until your mind and body function as one at the same instant.

The "in" condition is the one which makes you shine in performance, so you want to be sure to recognize it, as well as its absence. How do you get "in"? First of all, forget yourself. Focus on other people. Focus on the movement, on the quality of the movement, on the timing. Secondly, allow yourself to be swept along by the improvisation. Forget trying to do something clever and original. Third, try to get into your body the sensation of the dominant quality of the improvisational moment.

By forcing you to "think" on your feet, often before other people, improvisation develops your performance awareness. You are required to become aware not only of what you are experiencing at the moment, but also of the need to communicate that experience to an audience by your performance. Awareness of total environment includes other dancers, so a valuable feeling of rapport with them is gained through group improvisation.

2b. Improvisation can attain art status. Finally, improvisation may be an artistic end in itself. Its performance before an audience may be fully as satisfying as a finished piece of choreography. In the beginning, your improvisations will contain a lot of deadwood. They will be full of movement clichés, dynamically dull, trite and obvious. They will also contain tremendously exciting moments when you discover a movement for the first time, when some motion or relationship creates a moment of aesthetic delight or when an audience sees a movement for the first time. As you became more skilled at improvisation, the percentage of deadwood decreases and the moments of delight increase. Your developing intuition tells you the right thing to do at the right time. At this point, your improvisation is a spontaneous work of art. It has a real sense of wholeness; it begins, continues in a certain direction and reaches its own logical conclusion. Within each part, there is a sensitive use of motional elements. There is apparent form and a sensed meaning. When it satisfies all these qualifications, it can be said to be art.

3. Improvisation occurs simply by being allowed to happen.

No one can tell you *how* to improvise. No two improvisations are ever alike, so there is no pat formula you can follow. There are certain areas which you should leave open to the experience, though—your senses, your intuition and your memory.

Improvisation requires a degree of subjugation of your own will to the development of the improvisation in the way which is right for it. Your intuition is the only way you have of knowing that rightness. Thinking ahead intellectually is disastrous in improvisation, as it immediately destroys the spontaneity of the action and shows up visibly in the body as something "out" of key.

Although you give your conscious control over to the improvisation, you must not lose conscious awareness of your own response. This is perhaps the most important part of improvisation —your sensing of the experience. Be aware of your feeling for the whole experience, and encourage this by allowing yourself to become a part of it. Begin at the beginning, let the improvisation develop and end it when you feel as though nothing more should happen. Later, the memory of that sensed experience can be applied to other situations. Develop the skill of recall, as it is important when improvising prior to composition. You may improvise the most stunning movements in the world, but if you cannot recall them they are lost forever.

4. Group improvisation is personally and choreographically enriching.

You will need to do a great deal of improvisation alone to discover your own body and your own imagination without the distraction of other dancers. You will also do a lot of improvisation in a group. In this, your major task is to relate to the group as you apply yourselves together to the subject. You relate by being extraordinarily aware of the other dancers and the total environment at all times. You are alert for dynamic changes, for motional changes, for quality changes and for changes in any and all of the abstract elements of dance. You relate to these changes either by going along with them in a similar vein or by moving in contrast to them. There is never any one right way to respond, but there are some ways which are better than others, so you should learn to recognize them. Seize opportunities to make relationships, but do not force them.

Although you often give over your will to the group, you need not always be a follower. When you sense that a motion or a relationship has gone on too long or is becoming a bore, you may change it and start something else. Others will probably follow your lead if your intuition was right. If you find yourself alone in left field, you have probably misjudged. Lose yourself in the improvisation once more, and better luck next time.

As you improvise for each other in class, you can learn a great deal from watching. Look for those things which are particularly exciting, interesting and meaningful. Look for what pulls the improvisation together, and look for weak or dull parts. Be aware of contrasts. Were they effective? Too soon? Too much? Did one thing go on too long without variation? Did you see relationships between parts of the whole?

5. Motivations for improvisation are as extensive as life.

The subject matter for improvisation is limitless, ranging from the essence of owl to the closeness of a group in space, from the essence of adolescence to the mutual support of two dancers. In previous experiences, you have improvised with your body instrument and with the abstract elements of dance. Besides these two important areas, there is another source of dance material. This is the *environment* in which dance exists, and this can serve as the motivation for choreography as well as the final housing for performance.

In the natural experience of the human being, there are continual motor reactions, responses and adjustments to environment —to lights, sounds, objects and colors—as well as to other human beings in the environment. These responses are just as meaningful as those made to space, time and energy elements. Therefore, it is natural for choreographies to grow out of movement relating to any aspect of environment. You might build a dance on the way you could move in a particular costume, in a particular light or in a special set. Each of these elements will impose certain limitations because of its size, shape, color, intensity or weight, and will call for a kind of movement which is new and fascinating in itself. For instance, you might start a dance by carrying a long pole and develop a piece out of the relationship of your body to the pole. You might find out how you could move with respect to its function, shape, size and particular mobility. Here the "idea" of the dance becomes one of your relationship to your physical environment, discovered by your personal moving involvement with it.

Improvisations with these aspects make you at least five times more aware of the world around you. The following improvisations are designed to acquaint you with this environment outside yourself. They will, hopefully, suggest other ideas to you for your own improvisations or dances.

LEARNING EXPERIENCES—WITH SETS

Discover the shape, size, weight, color and form of a chair. Shape your body to conform to its design while sitting on the chair. Assume the shape of the chair in other places in space, without using the chair. Find many sitting positions on the chair. Choose four of these and move from one to another, varying fast and slow actions and transitions.

Discover new ways to move around, under, over and through the chair. How can the chair move? What are its other possible relationships to the floor? How can you move through space with the chair? (See the preceding left-hand photograph.)

Build an arrangement, or even a structure, of several chairs. Working with a group, fit yourselves into this arrangement and find new possibilities in the relationships between people and chairs.

Build a structural arrangement of boxes, platforms, ladders, chairs or similar objects. Explore movement in and among these objects. Discover the movement potential of the objects. Add other people, and keep them in mind as another element in the total relationship.

Build another architecture of functional objects, as above. People it with dancers who are free not only to move within the structure, but to change its arrangement as they see fit. Relate to the changing environment and to the other dancers.

WITH COSTUMES

Move across a space, pulling behind you 15 feet of rayon jersey material. Feel its weight, length and texture. Let your motion be consonant with the qualities of the cloth. Wear the cloth, roll in it and let it move as a result of your motion. Treat it as an extension of you, and not as a separate object.

Work in different kinds of costumes: skirts, pillow cases, beach towels, shoes, hats and other items. Discover the new entity made by you and the costume. Improvise with the costume as a part of you. (See the middle photograph.)

WITH PROPS

Improvise with a large garment bag. Discover what movement is possible within it. Be aware of the sounds created as you move. Try to visualize what is happening from the outside.

Move with a number of functional objects: suitcases, shovels, ladders, toothpicks and other items. Forget the specific functions of these objects and use them abstractly, responding to their size, shape, weight or texture.

Improvise with an abstract prop which has no recognizable function.

WITH SOUND

Start a movement sequence with a lift and drop of an arm or leg, followed by a sharp twist. Repeat it, in new directions and with new parts of your body. As you move, be aware of the sounds that accompany the motion because of the way you are forced to breathe or the squeak of your feet on the floor. Exaggerate these sounds and extend them to fill the duration of your movement sequence.

Explore sounds your body can make: snaps, claps, brushes, clicks or stamps. There is movement necessary to create these sounds. Explore vocal sounds, and move in agreement with them. Finally, discover what sounds are available from objects in the room, and the motion necessary to make them. Improvise in a group, relating to each other in sound and motion.

Use words or nonsense syllables for their sound value, and not for any literal meaning they may have. Improvise in a group, using verbalization as accompaniment.

Improvise, using recorded electronic music (such as Varèse's Poème électronique) as motivation. Allow the individual sounds to motivate movement. Then move to the more generally sensed essence of the piece. Maintain the movements and their quality, and try them again to a completely different kind of musical background. Be aware of the resultant feeling.

WITH PEOPLE

You may have found that your reaction to other people is one of the most fascinating factors in improvisation and that interrelationships between people can produce the most meaningful materials for choreography. Other people are perhaps the most important influence on us in our daily life, so their significance for dance is only natural. It is important to develop added sensitivity to others in movement situations.

Watch individual people as they sit, stand and walk, and attempt to imitate them exactly in order to increase your awareness of the characteristic movement styles of others in your group.

Work with a partner. Face each other as you would your reflection in a mirror. Establish a line between you to represent that mirror. Improvise slowly, being sensitive to the shapes being made, to your relative distances from the mirror and to the fidelity with which you reflect each other's image. Let the initiation of movement pass from partner to partner, with no verbal communication. Try to move simultaneously.

Working with a partner, improvise on the premise that you must maintain physical contact at some point throughout the improvisation. The contact point may change, but try to explore the possibilities of each one thoroughly before changing. Begin with your eyes closed, and sense each other without the aid of your vision. When you are sufficiently tuned in to one another, open your eyes and continue. (See the preceding right-hand photograph.)

In groups of threes, begin in a relationship with contact. Hold your position until something has to move. Let the improvisation proceed from that first impulse, into whatever is possible and special for groups of three. Allow it to stop when it is finished.

Standing in a circle, make contact somehow with those on each side and hold the position of contact. As weights and pulls become noticeable, allow yourself to go in the direction indicated, but gently and carefully, so as not to destroy the circle. Let the improvisation unfold until it comes to a natural end.

Standing in a closely packed group so that all are somehow touching while facing forward, tune in to the group pulse. Be aware of the lift and fall of breathing bodies. Be aware of the natural postural sway and do not restrain it. When you feel pressures on your body, allow subtle changes in your own position to occur, and then be open to whatever may happen next. Try to be so sensitively attuned that the group moves as one body with one mind.

Design a group arrangement in which people are related in space because of the way they are facing; use only the four walls for directions. Improvise by merely walking or changing level. The body stays upright, movement can go only up and down or toward the walls, direction can change and one may travel forward, backward or sideways. Tempos also may vary. Be aware of the close interrelationship experienced here, and of the feeling of action-reaction which occurs.

Walking in a circle, watch and pick up the tempo and mannerisms of the walk of each person progressively. Then, focusing on no particular person, try to establish a group tempo. Change the tempo; speed it up; slow it down; try to let it happen as a group phenomenon, rather than as the result of any one person's action.

Finally, begin with an environment of objects in space; add sound, light, people and costumes, and stir. Let the "stew" evolve as it will.

Concept V—Choreography Is the Creative Art Process in Dance

YOUR EXPERIENCES so far in the medium of movement and the elements of time, space and energy have been for the purposes of developing sensitivity and awareness and exploring the various materials of dance. The experiences can be viewed also as approaches to choreography. In completing the experiences and solving the movement problems so far presented, you have been going through the choreographic process in miniature. You have explored, improvised and set movement patterns that could be repeated. What remains is to expand each of these explorations, improvisations and patterns into dances of sufficient length and depth to satisfy you as a choreographer and others as audience.

1. Choreography involves the processes of exploration, improvisation, selection and organization.

You are already acquainted with these processes from your previous experiences. In *exploration,* you find ways to do that which you have already decided to do. For instance, if you want to do a study of "stop and go," you might explore all the ways of stopping and going that you can think of and then select from these the ways that best suit your purpose. Again, if you want to get from a low wide position to a high narrow one in the middle of a dance, you could explore all the ways possible until you found the way that was right, most effective, for your needs. Exploration goes on as a series of disconnected trials in search of material of a predetermined nature.

Improvisation is a spontaneous forming, a continuous sequential growth of movement and events out of the motivating idea. It is a process of letting things happen, rather than intellectually predetermining what will occur. From the improvisation, you may sense and remember things which you will use as movement and ideas for choreography. Improvisation can give you ways of developing already chosen materials or of progressing in sequences. It can present you with exciting shapes, rhythms and relationships which you will make use of or build on in choreography.

From your explorations and improvisations, you make a *selection* of material appropriate for dance. This selection can be based on intellectual reasoning, but more often it will simply come about intuitively. Reason has its place in science, but art is better served by intuition. You sense materials as important and you feel an order of movement as inevitable.

Finally, you will organize movement, sequences and relationships according to what seems to be the right progression for your dance. The most careful and adequate forming of the dance will come only out of the most thorough acquaintance with the movement materials. Many times initial movements will have inherent in them the form for the whole dance. The organization of a dance can come about by an intellectual choice and ordering of parts. It can come about organically, with movement growing naturally out of previous movement in a sequential development. Or, it can come about as a combination of these two methods. You will develop form by intuition, by your sensing of the way the dance should progress. You might also develop form by chance, by selecting a possibility out of a hatful of choices.

Organization implies more than just arbitrarily stringing movements together. You will work, arrange and rearrange, improvise and explore, combine and recombine until you find a sequence which makes a kind of nonverbalizable sense to you. It implies that you have made the connection between movement and some kind of meaning that this movement has for you, and the meaning is developed and extended by this particular order of movement. The movement is no longer sensed purely in its mechanics, but has meaning for you, makes you feel a certain way.

2. Choreographing is a way of getting to know yourself.

Your work as a composer of dances cannot begin too early, and should never be saved until you think that your technical development is complete. Make your mistakes in composition early, and profit from them. Each movement study you choreograph teaches you a new lesson, not only about composition, but also about the body you inhabit. Choreography is just as important for technical growth as it is for creative growth. You will demand certain skills of yourself to satisfy your choreography, and will possibly be harder on yourself than anyone else will be.

3. Determination of motivation, material and method facilitates the choreographic process and clarifies the product.

Whether you are choreographing for one dancer or for many, you will find these things to be true: first, you need a motivation for the dance. In class, this may be as simple as being told by your instructor to create a dance. This assignment may be further qualified by specific limits as to subject, length, quality and other details. You may simply have an inner need to choreograph a dance, and be self-directed in accomplishing it. In any case, whether the motivation comes from an inside or outside source, you have an image or thought about the dance. You may be able to put your thought into words, or it may be nonverbal, coming to life only in movement. You improvise for movement materials which form it for you. Consequently, you have an idea about how that thought might manifest itself in movement. How many dancers will it need? What speed? What dynamics? What quality have you discovered or decided upon? Finally, you decide on how best to start working so that your image will take shape. The method of working strongly influences the final form of the dance, as each dance takes its own unique form. Some dances will follow a predetermined, literal course. There may be a comment that you want to make. This requires much intellectual work. Other dances will begin and grow and form mostly through the interaction of intuition and movement. Some will be suitable for only one person, others will require a group to best create their effect. There are as many possible approaches and procedures with choreography as there are choreographers and dances.

   3a. The method of working in solo choreography is determined by its motivation. You may design your dances as solos, either for yourself or for a dancer who seems to have the potential capacity to give what is needed to your dance and with whom you have good rapport. There are special things to be considered when choreographing for a solo dancer. You need to keep in mind that the single dancer must maintain consistent interest so as to hold the stage without monotony throughout the length of the dance. This means more complex movement than would be advisable in a group dance, and more careful selection of pungent moments of movement.

In working on a solo, it is very tempting for the choreographer to overuse the mirror because there are no other dancers on whom one can see the movement. This can be a dangerous procedure. Mirror-fed minds tend to deal mainly with shape, to the exclusion of other equally important elements such as motion, speed and space. This crutchlike dependence on the mirror is the result of an attempt to get outside yourself to see what the movement looks like. Try instead to get outside yourself kinesthetically —that is, to know through muscle sensation what you look like visually.

The *free improvisation* method of composing starts from the broadest possible base and works toward the more specific. This is one way to start when you have no more concrete vision than the fact that you want to do a dance, or that you simply want to move. You begin by improvising freely, with no limitations, until some motion, shape, feeling or other quality arrests you. That is your beginning, your seed from which the dance will grow. You continue improvising, selecting motion that seems to work and to be in harmony with the beginning seed.

When you work with a *limited problem,* already having a vision in mind, whether it be your own creation or an assigned exercise, you have a more specific basis from which to start composing. Choosing a quality of movement on which to concentrate automatically eliminates many others. Consequently, your preliminary improvisation is shortened because it is more specifically directed toward your vision. As in the method above, you try and discard, and finally select, movements which are true to your image—which keep the quality without reiterating it to the point of boredom. The stronger your image to begin with, the more quickly the composition will fall into place. Be open, however, to the possibility of your vision altering before your very mind's eye. This frequently happens—an accidental occurrence may prove more interesting than the original idea. If this should happen, do not hesitate to drop the first and pursue the second. Dance compositions, like improvisations, seem to have a will of their own, and sometimes they simply will not be forced. If you let them develop naturally, you are more likely to end with a complete, organic dance.

Often something apart from dance itself, some outside stimulus, will start the spark of creativity burning. Sometimes it is a particular sound or accompaniment which might lend itself well to dance. Sometimes it is a prop or a costume or an unusual physical environment. These considerations narrow the limits in which you have to work, but they also may make things more difficult for you. Because they constitute an influence that is in a way limiting to the motion, the dance will have to conform to that limitation. It can no longer go its merry way without relating to the thing which brought it into being in the first place.

If your idea requires greater numbers of people to make its statement, there will be greater possibilities for building, for contrast, for harmony, for saying many things more powerfully than a single dancer can do, and perhaps even greater problems. There are at least several considerations necessary in working with a group.

The more people in your group dance, the more you need to simplify the choreography. A movement is amplified in proportion to the number of people doing it. If 20 people on a stage are all doing something different, no one movement will stand out, and the viewer may be hopelessly confused. A group dance, then, needs careful pruning of extraneous movements so that the ones which are kept say very clearly what you wish them to say.

For the less experienced choreographer, it is a wise move to stay out of the group dance you are composing—or, if you must dance in it, get someone else to take your place during rehearsal so you can back off from the dance and see what is happening. In this capacity you serve as the "outside eye," and are better able to judge the workability of each phrase than you would be if you were in the midst of it. The "outside eye" is even more of a necessity in a group dance than in a solo, due to the complexity of spatial relationships and the impossibility of kinesthetically sensing anyone's movement but your own.

3b. The motivation of the dance determines method and materials for a group choreography. In *free improvisation,* you simply turn your dancers loose with instructions to improvise on no particular subject, and wait for something to happen. When it does, seize the moment and try to have your dancers repeat it. If they can, and you like it, then you have a seed around which the rest of the dance can build. The dancers then continue to improvise with an image in mind of what they are working toward, and hopefully the dance goes on. This is probably the most haphazard way to work, and is usually most successful with experienced improvisers. It takes a while to get "tuned in" to a group; and even when things begin working, it is difficult to recall and reproduce them. It can be a very exciting way to work, however, as the resultant dance is often as much of a surprise to the choreographer as it is to anyone else.

Setting a *skeleton problem* uses improvisation, too, but this is a little more directed than the preceding way. You, as the choreographer, have an image of what you would like to see and, as well as you are able, try to communicate this image to the dancers. They then have some framework around which to begin improvising—some straw in the wind to which they can cling. As before, you then select the moments that seem to fit in with your image, ask your dancers to recall them and gradually set them into a firm sequence. The more clearly you can describe your image, the less time will be wasted as your dancers try to discover what it is you want from them. (For all these improvisational methods, the ideal technical device to have is an instant-playback television set.)

Still more closely directed is the *partial improvisation,* in which you give your dancers prepared sequences of movement, but also allow them sections in which to improvise. You establish the quality of the movement you would like to see, and they may improvise with it in time, space and dynamics. In the finished dance, these sections may still be improvised to some degree, or they may gel during rehearsal so that they are nearly always performed in the same way.

In the *totally structured* way of working, you give your dancers every movement they are to do, in the sequences in which they are to be done. There is no room for improvisation; the dancers just learn what you are teaching. This, of course, necessitates a great deal of work on your part prior to rehearsals with your dancers, so that you are sure to have something to give them. You will have gone through the improvisation, exploration and selection process yourself before confronting them. Although the forming process may occur when and as you see the movements being danced and can determine an order, it would be grossly unfair for you to ask dancers to stand around and wait while you think about the basic materials. Presenting a set structure often saves time in rehearsals, but it cannot take advantage of the spontaneous moments that often happen in improvisation.

Try many different methods of working. Although you may ultimately find one or two that are more suitable to you, you will gain from the experience of trying them all.

4. Choreographic process is individual to each choreographer and each dance.

What has been said is about all anyone can tell you about the making of dances. There is no set of rules, no progression of steps, not even an order of processes that anyone can recommend to you as those that will work each time. How you proceed will be a matter of your own intuition and your own sense of rightness.

You will work intuitively or intellectually, and probably some of each. You will work subjectively or objectively, sometimes being in the movement, involved only in its feel, and other times out of it, trying to see it from the point of view of the observer. You may discover that if you preplan and decide ahead of the movement what and how you are going to move, you will limit your spontaneity and the ease with which the movement flows. You may also miss the opportunity to discover something brand new that just happens to you without anticipation. You will discover at what point in the process you must look at your work objectively, to give it direction, to see what it is you have and how you can progress—to define the basis on which you will keep or throw materials away. You will find at what point you can do this without its being a detriment to the spontaneity and flow of your work, and at what point you must do this or lose the form of the dance to unrelated wanderings because you have not yet defined your direction.

4a. Developing discrimination facilitates the process of choreography. You will grow tremendously in awareness and intuition as you do, see and evaluate your own and others' choreographies. The more experience you have, the more discriminating you will become.

You will have already sensed your own studies as exciting, as important to you in some way, or somehow lacking in the essential qualities. You will have seen and evaluated other studies. Hopefully, you will have sensed for yourself and discussed as a group what it is about these studies that you like, what you consider good, exciting and stimulating, and why certain studies are dull, ordinary and not so exciting or meaningful. Perhaps you have had insights into the "whys" of a thing being new and fresh, captivating and moving, creative and original, completely absorbing. From these insights, you should be better able to find those qualities for yourself in your own dances.

The difference between the genius and the ordinary person is not in the size or chemistry of his brain structure, but in the intensity of his desire, concentration and willpower. The important thing is that you do, that you choreograph, that you make dances; and that you continue to evaluate your experiences, your dances and the dances of others, and to learn from your own reactions and those of others how you can better or more effectively fulfill your dance ideas.

4b. Experiences in other art media will enhance your work in choreography. While you are working and learning, you may want to surround yourself with other art products and immerse yourself in other art experiences. Read what Martha Graham and Mary Wigman have to say about their choreographic experiences. Read what other artists in other areas have written about their creative processes. Picasso and Paul Klee are articulate in their descriptions. Giocometti mentions the occasional frustration and lack of surety all artists experience. Be comforted. Brewster Ghiselin's *The Creative Process* relates the experiences of artists and scientists in the act of creating. Read and reread them, for what they say may not make sense to you just now, while at another stage in your development it may be as clear to you as dawn.

Talk to other people going through the same processes and problems. Listen to what your instructor has to suggest to you. You will sort out from their insights things which contribute to your understanding. Attend concerts and plays, listen to music, read poetry and visit museums. Experience fully, and later reflect on your feeling sensations and try to understand them. You might try the following:

LEARNING EXPERIENCES

Begin with Martha Graham's dance film, Night Journey, *and study carefully the structure of the story of Jocasta. What function does the chorus serve? What is the effect of the seer? How are all the parts unified, not only in story line, but in movement? In costume, set, and prop? How is each part related to the others?*

Attend a concert of Alwin Nikolais, or watch one of his television films. Experience the sensory magic of motion, sound, light and color in a theatrical whole. In what ways is his work different from that of Graham?

See, experience and evaluate as much dance as you can and, most important, do your own choreography. Choreograph continually, a study a day if possible; it is like practicing anything in which you would like to acquire skill. At this point, you must take full responsibility for yourself and your work, you must learn through painful trials and errors, through jubilant revelations and insights. The amount of experience you have in dance is equivalent to the amount you will grow. This is up to you.

Each of you will eventually find your own way of proceeding. You will set your own individual problems, decide on your own ideas or first movement, find your own method of approaching choreography and progressing, and define a standard of taste. Then, lo and behold, once you think you have found the way, you will discover that each dance has a mind of its own, and that you have changed a little in your ideas. This is the difficulty and frustration, the excitement and joy, of art. It is a process not yet scientifically understood or rationally explainable. It requires patience for, and tolerance of, its vagueness and obscurity. It will have its depressions and frustrations, its enlightenments and exaltations; all this you can truly anticipate. Have no illusions.

5. The dance is mounted in theatrical elements to enhance and emphasize the desired effect.

At a certain point in your development, you will be pleased enough with your choreography to consider it a worthwhile experience for an audience. You will be concerned with dance in its ultimate state—as a performing art. As an art, dance occurs in a particular environment, as mentioned previously. Environment refers to all the theatrical elements which make up the total presentation on a stage—the costumes, props, sets, lights, accompaniment and program titles. They are those elements which heighten the experience for the viewer. They provide the magic of the stage that helps to create the illusion necessary for the art to exist as other than everyday activity. In the theatre situation, they support and intensify the dance idea.

5a. Theatrical elements serve to enrich the experience of the viewer through an increase in sense activity. Lights will ensure the seeing of the right images, support the mood in rays and colors, help to isolate or pull together, to lift, press down or emphasize. Sets have a significance for the dance design. They change its shape in space, supply mass, bulk, shape and texture, intensifying or adding contrast to those already present in the movement. Props are often necessary in carrying out the full meaning of the dance. Perhaps more often they serve to extend movement lines and shapes and to emphasize qualities. When props and sets are used symbolically, they are used in the sense of drama. As such, they require additional interpretive thought on the part of the viewer. This may detract from his involvement with and his enjoyment of the experience of motion. Keep this in mind if you choose to use props in this way.

Costumes, while identifying period and character in drama, serve in dance more to extend the quality of a movement or accentuate parts of the body. They have the potential to create line and shape, to provide interest through their texture and color, and to support movement definitions in their line, weight and motional qualities. They not only emphasize visual aspects, but many times provide sensations of touch through their texture and weight, thus involving a fuller sensuous response of the audience.

Music or sound accompaniment stimulates a third sense—hearing. It can intensify a mood or create an aural atmosphere in which dance can happen. It can, if the choreographer desires, even produce a sense of conflict by being opposite to the timing or quality of the dance. In giving an auditory dimension to the sensory experience of the dance, it further enriches and deepens it.

None of these elements are things which should be added after the dance is completely formulated, however. They are conceived along with the dance, as an integral part of it. They must be organically necessary to the totality of the work. These elements actually affect the movement, so you must work with them in the process of learning and choreographing the dance. If this is not done, the dance may suddenly change when you add other elements. These elements should facilitate, and not oppose, the desired effect.

5b. Sound, in particular, is influential in the effectiveness of the dance. Of all the elements, music is probably the most important in its influence on not only the dancers and audience, but also on the dance. It has the power to change the overall effect of the dance, and to irritate or to soothe the audience as it experiences the dance. In searching for dance accompaniment, then, be careful to find something suitable, something similar in mood and time to your dance. Take plenty of time to listen, and be willing to wait for that which is *most* effective. As in your choice of movement for dance, don't be too easily satisfied.

It would be nice to have music written for your choreographies, but that presents special problems of its own and is not usually possible in the school situation. Nevertheless, you may be lucky enough to find faculty or students in your music department who would welcome the chance to compose for dance. Many times, they feel it extends them in their vocabulary of sound and rhythm. You can at least talk to the music department people about the particular sound needs for your choreography. Oftentimes, they can suggest just the right composer or piece to meet your style, time and tensional requirements. Don't hesitate to listen to their record library, visit record stores and listen there, and tune your radio to good music. Your familiarity with what is available will greatly facilitate the selection of accompaniment.

There may be times when it seems much easier simply to put a record on the phonograph and dance to it. This is good therapy, and you may even come up with something worthwhile by following the music's rhythms and form, or by being excited by its mood. This excitement, however, comes from an external motivation rather than from your own inner motor impulse. Here the dance accompanies the music, rather than the other, more desirable way around. Some music, of course, is not too adaptable. Many pieces are so complete and powerful in themselves that a dance does little more than irritate by distracting from the music. Even professional companies have trouble being adequate to Bach masses, which are already adequate in themselves.

Do not overlook the possibilities of using nonmusical sounds such as voice, words, percussion, electronic sound and even everyday noises for accompaniment. Their looser structure sometimes allows greater freedom in combining sound and movement.

5c. The title of a dance in the program is very influential in affecting audience reaction. With the choreography complete, and its staging planned, what will you call your dance? This can be a problem. Your title can mislead the viewer, as well as help him in understanding your dance. If there is something specific that you as a choreographer want to get across, perhaps you will insist that your audience see this in the dance. You will title it accordingly, giving people a point of view from which to see the dance. In this case, there are problems. If the title is definitive, it may lead the viewer to expect certain definite things, because of his personal associations. He may be disappointed in your interpretation, or he may be distracted from the movement by searching for the representation of the idea. He may never see the dance if he is so busy intellectually trying to figure it out in relation to its title. This is probably why so many modern artists are content with titles like *Study in Blue* or *Number 7*. Here the observer is free to let his own imagination loose, and is not trapped into trying to find something which just isn't there. Usually, one doesn't ask of *Symphony No. 9*, "What is your meaning?" It is enough simply to enjoy the sound, harmonies and structure.

Since most dance deals with nonliteral things and with movement ideas, choreographers often give titles of implication, of suggestion or atmosphere, as possible springboards to send the imagination of the viewer into this particular experience of movement. Perhaps it is better if a title simply identifies a dance, as a name identifies a person. What set of words can possibly contain a human personality or the motional content of a choreography?

Concept VI—Performance Is the Final Step in the Choreographic Process

ONCE THE DANCE is formulated and rehearsed, it will be shown, as the purpose of dance is to share it with others. Granted, there is tremendous self-satisfaction in creating choreography, but dance is by nature a performing art and fulfills its true function only when presented before people. Certainly you may dance just for your own enjoyment, but ultimately you will perform, whether it be for your own classmates, for your instructor or for a theatre audience. To these people you have certain responsibilities, both as a dancer and as a choreographer. You are dealing with art, and this automatically means that your standards are high. They should be no different from those of the professional—to present the best work of which you are capable.

One can say that a dance is a series of transactions. The series begins with the experienced or imagined feeling of the choreographer. It is felt as a kind of restless excitement until given a plan of motion. This vision is given substance and visual existence by the dancer. It is the dance which is the link between the choreographer and the dancer, and between the dancer and his audience. And the audience, of course, is the final link in the chain.

1. The presence of an audience demands the greatest fulfillment of the performance.

1a. The nature of the audience affects the existence of the choreography. The people in your audience arrive at your performance in various states of mind, and they see different things in that performance. They bring minds accustomed to thinking verbally, and what you are presenting to them is an essentially nonverbal art. They may also bring ideas about what they expect to see. The more firmly fixed these ideas, the greater your chance of disappointing them if you do not deliver what they expect. They bring with them their lifetime collection of associations and memories and their habit of mentally organizing and connecting new experiences and meanings with those they have had in the past. They bring with them the tendency of the educated mind to search out literal meaning in everything it sees.

How ideal it would be if those minds in your audience were uncluttered by old associations and by pre-set ideas of excellence. You would like the audience to see your work clean and pure, without the judgment of their past experience hastening in upon it. The experience you bring them should be like the first marks on fresh snow. Unless you dance for day-old babies, this will never be the case. The next step, then, is to provide your audience with an experience that is as crystal-clear and new as possible, and hope it will move them past their prejudices.

1b. The choreographer has a responsibility to help the audience toward a new experience. Whether the audience be your own small group of friends or paying customers in a theatre, they have one thing in common. They expect to be stimulated in some way by what you do. Your responsibility as both a choreographer and performer is to see that they are stimulated. You may do this in a number of ways. You may arouse them emotionally, or you may provide them with a pleasant sensuous experience, give them some intellectual fodder, or even make them downright angry. The point is to give them an experience they have not had before.

The audience is responsive to the dance-theatre experience in a number of ways. The viewer is impressed visually with the shape, color and motion he sees on the stage. He is aware of sounds, whether they be accompanying sounds or the sounds the dancers themselves make. He also lives vicariously the motional experience of the dancer. He actually feels muscularly, to a slight degree, the same things the moving dancer is feeling.

These are essentially sensory responses to the dance experience. At the same time the viewer is probably responding intellectually too, dredging up those previously-mentioned past associations and trying to apply them to the present situation. Since dance is first a sensory experience, you may as a choreographer deal with the strictly sensory aspects of your work, and leave the intellectualizing to the audience. Since each viewer will react differently anyway, by virtue of having different past memories, there is nothing that would be universally applicable.

The choreographer's responsibility, then, is to clear the channels of any extraneous associations as much as possible, so that the viewer may have a new experience. This would mean avoiding anything which has a strong symbolic tie with the past—sentimental music, hackneyed postures of emotional states or recognized symbols like crosses, flags and other objects. By dealing with the abstract elements of his art, the choreographer leaves his audience free to enjoy the basic sensory experience, or to find their own meaning in it, be it abstract or literal. Abstract meaning is a perfectly valid and real outcome of dance. There are qualities of ideas and images which cannot be expressed verbally; these ideas *mean* abstractly, not literally.

1c. The dancer has a responsibility to give his audience a full and clear experience of the dance. The audience sees what the choreographer has to say through the dancer. As the dancer, you can best serve the choreographer and the audience by becoming transparent—by letting the choreography shine through you. When your ego intrudes—when the audience is more aware of "you, dancing" than it is of the motion itself, when you wear the movement like a decoration adorning your outer surface—then you clutter up the vision and the audience can no longer see the dance clearly.

On the other hand, you have a certain responsibility to be an ingratiating performer. Part of the viewer's pleasure is in identifying kinetically with the dancer in motion, and you will make this identification hard for him if you present a cold and austere or in some way negative figure. There is a delicate balance between selflessness and the denial of the self.

There is a danger of clouding the choreographic issue not only with the self, but also with dramatic attitudes imposed on the choreography. If there is drama in the choreography, it will be inherent in the movement. You will not have to slap it on like a final coat of paint. When you color a movement with an emotional attitude, you immediately direct the viewer's attention down a particular avenue of thought and rob him of the opportunity to explore other avenues.

Your foremost duty, then, is to present the choreography to the audience without editorial comment. Consider yourself, instead, as the vehicle which carries the choreography to the audience. By devotion to the motion and not to what you think the motion means, you eliminate the middle man and let the audience perceive the dance directly. The concept of the dancer as interpreter of the choreography implies that the choreographer is speaking in a language audiences cannot understand without a translator, and you have often heard that something always gets lost in the translation.

Performers have maintained from time immemorial that all audiences are different and that it is necessary to play to each differently. All this is certainly true. An audience of children is different from an audience of ladies' club members or an audience of other dancers. They will all react differently to you, and you to them. Because of the vast variations in audience composition, there is nothing that could begin to prepare you, the performer, for all the situations you may encounter. Sensing the make-up and mood of an audience is a skill that comes only after many, many performances before many types of audiences. It behooves you to seize every opportunity to perform, no matter if the performing conditions sound a little dismaying. Perhaps your greatest moment of growth will come when you have to adjust to dancing on a stage the size of a bath mat, in your practice tights because your costumes got lost, to the tune of the friendly janitor's kazoo because your tape recorder broke down, for an audience of six.

Performance nerves—or in plain English, fear—is always present to some degree, and it can be either crippling or stimulating. It may so shatter you that your physical and psychical control are destroyed, or it may sharpen your energies and sensitivities so that you give the performance of your lifetime. Again, only repeated performances will teach you to deal with this problem, and no one can give you any really helpful advice on how to meet it. One can only say that the stress of performance intensifies everything. Turn your concentration to careful articulation of the motion, rather than to yourself, your nerves and fears, and it will be motion that will be magnified for the audience—not your shaking knees.

An easiness in the face may help you to develop calmness. If you are unaccustomed to wearing a pleasant, open face when you dance, then you had better practice it. The mirror will show you the difference between a closed face and a toothy grin. Use rehearsal time for this; the night of the performance is a little late to begin. You simply have to concentrate on too many other things.

What if you make a mistake? Or even fall down? Quite honestly, the world will not come to an immediate halt. The important thing is to spare the audience the discomfort of your embarrassment. The audience is simply not interested in seeing your fears or your remorse. An attitude of confidence in performing can not only set you up in a frame of mind to help you deliver a good performance, but it can also smooth over any hitches that may occur.

1d. The theatre situation must be clarified to provide the most magical experience for the viewer. The physical environment for dancing certainly influences the effect of the performance. In actual performance, the technical details of light and sound, hopefully, will be taken care of by at least one other person whose responsibility it is to see that all these things work properly. It is important that you, as a dancer or choreographer, find a capable, responsible, sensitive person to stage your dance, and to make it perfectly plain to this person exactly what you want. To ensure the best result, communicate with him in his own language. Know and use the proper terminologies for lights, sets and directions on stage. Once these technical details are established and under his control, you can forget about them and concentrate on what you, the dancer, can do with your performing environment.

The stage space may seem a fixed element to you, but it is really most hospitable to change. You are capable of altering the appearance of that space by the manner in which you treat it. (See Concept III.) A small stage can be made to seem infinite if you project your movement out beyond the space around you. You can do this through eye focus, through subtle extensions of motion and through extension of the psyche. You can make the illusion of space that you create crash through the walls which enclose that tiny stage. Or, because of the nature of the dance, you may wish to play the movement in proportion to the actual size of the stage. This may mean treating it more intimately and inviting the audience "in" to the space, rather than projecting it out to them.

On the other hand, a large stage may be treated projectionally to take advantage of its spaciousness, or to tone it down if the space is such that it overwhelms your dance. By your focus on the motion, you may either send it out into the space or illusionally pull the boundaries of that space down to manageable size.

In any case, your audience will see what you want it to see, if you have sufficient skill. They may see a real space expand or contract. They may see a space with a density as thick as glue, or as thin as outer space. You control the space, so to a great degree, you control what the audience sees.

2. Dancers have a responsibility to each other to realize a coordinated effort and effect.

Unless you plan to dance nothing but solos all your life, you will often find yourself a member of a group dance. In order to preserve sanity and make the experience as pleasant as possible for all concerned, you will want to be mindful of your responsibility to your fellow dancers.

The rehearsals will be the most trying times, particularly the early ones when the dance is beginning to take shape. Approach each rehearsal professionally, even though you may not be a professional yet. Come to the rehearsal sufficiently early to get your mind and body ready to work. Warm up your instrument and be ready to begin at the time set. Learn to discipline yourself to work during the time set aside for it. Wasting other people's time is inexcusable. If you have spatial problems with other dancers, or if there is a movement discrepancy, work these problems out efficiently, pleasantly, and preferably on your own, not the choreographer's, time.

Always try to rehearse "full out"—that is, just as you intend to perform, with every motion getting its full complement of energy. Not only will this build your physical stamina, but it will also heighten your own familiarity with the dynamics. You cannot "mark" through every rehearsal and expect to know how to execute the movement dynamically in performance. In addition, other dancers are taking energy cues from you, and it is impossible to achieve any kind of group rapport if there is one dead spot on the stage.

Finally, the business of group rapport is probably the most important of all, and you must work at it constantly. It is a state of awareness of the total environment and a communication that exists between the dancers, almost like a charge of electricity. You are sensitive to the motion, the timing and the dynamics of the other dancers, and you adjust your own accordingly. If you fail to do so, you stand out as a jarring note that seems incongruous with the rest of the ensemble. When you are in this state of almost telepathic communication, you are ready for any untoward event.

3. The dancer has the responsibility to be the instrument of the choreographer.

Choreographers work in different ways, and hopefully you will have the opportunity to work with many of them. Though you are the raw material with which the choreographer works, and therefore subject to his will, your duties go beyond just appearing at rehearsal to "do the steps." The extent of your contribution will vary according to the way the choreographer works. If he wishes you to improvise around an idea, do so with all your creative skill. If he gives you every movement in the dance and expects to see the movements reproduced exactly, do so with accuracy. If he asks for your suggestions, feel free to give them—constructively, of course. Ultimately, the responsibility for the success or failure of the work is on the choreographer's shoulders. Although you may think his judgment wrong, it is not your place to correct him. You are his instrument, not his conscience.

Try to keep your body and spirit alive and your energy up throughout the rehearsal, no matter how tired you may be. A "full out" rehearsal of a movement is doubly important to the choreographer, as he cannot really see if a movement works if it is not fulfilled dynamically.

Once you have learned the movement, your work is just beginning. In the studio alone, you spend hours with yourself and with the choreography. You examine each movement to see what its character is—what quality to bring out in performance. You discover where the phrases break naturally. You find the climax of the entire piece. You practice subtleties of performance, nuances that distinguish the dancer from the hack.

You perform. You make the vision that was in the mind of the choreographer come alive. You allow the audience to see through you to the choreography, to the motion. If you can do this, then you have faithfully discharged your duty to the choreographer.

4. The dancer has the responsibility of integrity in recreating the dance.

When the final moment of truth, the performance, comes, the dancer is left with two things—himself and the choreography. Let there be no mistake as to which is the more important. A dedicated giving over of one's self to the movement is necessary to involve the audience directly in the choreography. It is only by total devotion to the motion, and to the quality therein, that a dancer can make a clear communication of the material to his audience.

5. The dancer may have the privilege of pleasing the audience.

You have come to the final link in the series of transactions. You present the dance. The audience receives it; and it goes one step further. The audience doesn't just take the experience in and keep it. There is a response, sometimes very subtle, but a response—a particular kind of energy which is produced and generated back to the dancer. It happens sometimes like refrigeration, sometimes like lukewarm water, and sometimes—if you are very lucky—like the radiance of open love and acceptance. It is for that moment that you wait.

LEARNING EXPERIENCES

1. *See and experience a modern dance concert, of professional level if possible, and write a critique of it, evaluating and discussing it in terms of points mentioned in this section on performance.*

2. *Choreograph and perform a dance for an audience. Evaluate the experience from your point of view—from that of the audience.*

Concept VII—The Dance Experience Is Synonymous with Growth

THE END OF this course may mark the end of your personal contact with dance or the beginning of a rewarding pursuit of dance, either as participant or spectator. Whether you continue to dance is not the main point. The point is that you are not the same person you were at the beginning of this course.

You cannot be the same because you have had new experiences —experiences in moving, in seeing, in creating. You have felt the stretch of a muscle, the torsion of a twist, the sensation of weight and the fatigue of a muscle used to its capacity. You know how it feels to be upside down, to run and stop and to be dizzy from turning.

You turned to your creative resources and found them capable of originality. You dug inside yourself and found ideas, gave those ideas physical form and showed those forms to someone else.

You have had new experiences in seeing, because new knowledge changes the way you see. You have learned to see spatially— in line, shape and mass. You have learned to see time—its duration and its speed. You have tuned your eyes to those abstract qualities which make up motion, which make up your world. You have seen other people, other dancers and other dances. You have seen yourself from the inside out and the outside in.

In short, you know yourself and your world a little better, and you know what it is to dance.

Concept VIII—When Growth Overcomes Inertia, It Sets Up a Momentum Difficult to Stop

HERE IS A bibliography for your further enrichment:

Periodicals:

Dance Magazine (monthly), 268 West 47th St., New York 36, N.Y.

Dance Perspectives (quarterly), 1801 East 26th St., Brooklyn 29, N.Y.

Impulse (annual), Impulse Publications, Inc., 160 Palo Alto Ave., San Francisco, Calif.

Dance Scope (semi-annual), National Dance Teachers Guild, Inc., 124–16 84th Rd., Kew Gardens, N.Y. 11415.

Readings in Dance:

Cohen, Selma Jean, ed. *The Modern Dance, Seven Statements of Belief.* Middletown, Conn.: Wesleyan University Press, 1966.

DeMille, Agnes. *Lizzie Borden: A Dance of Death.* Boston: Little, Brown & Co., 1968.

Ellfeldt, Lois. *A Primer for Choreographers.* Palo Alto, Calif.: National Press Books, 1967.

Horst, Louis, and Russell, Carroll. *Modern Dance Forms.* San Francisco: Impulse Publications, Inc., 1961.

Martin, John. *Book of the Dance.* New York: Tudor Publishing Co., 1963.

———. *The Modern Dance.* New York: Dance Horizons, Inc., 1933 (reprint).

Sorrell, Walter. *The Dance Through the Ages.* New York: Grosset & Dunlap, 1967.

Wigman, Mary. *The Language of Dance.* Middletown, Conn.: Wesleyan University Press, 1966.

Books in Related Areas:

Ghiselin, Brewster, ed. *The Creative Process: A Symposium.* Berkeley, Calif.: University of California Press, 1952.

Gilot, Francoise, and Lake, Carlton. *Life with Picasso.* New York: The New American Library, 1964.

Lord, James. *A Giacometti Portrait.* New York: The Museum of Modern Art, distributed by Doubleday & Company, Inc., 1964.

Lynton, Norbert. *Klee.* London: Spring Books, 1964.

Allyn and Bacon Series in
BASIC CONCEPTS OF PHYSICAL ACTIVITY

Consulting Editors:
Raymond A. Snyder, *U. of Cal., Los Angeles*
Thomas W. Evaul, *Temple University*

RELATED TITLES AVAILABLE NOW

GOLF
Bruce Fossum, *Mich. State U.*
Mary Dagraedt, *Miami-Dade Junior College*

WOMEN'S GYMNASTICS
Kitty Kjeldsen, *U. of Mass.*

VOLLEYBALL
Allen E. Scates, *U. of Cal., Los Angeles*
Jane Ward, *Cabrillo College, Aptos, Cal.*

BODY CONTOURING AND CONDITIONING THROUGH MOVEMENT
Janet Wessel, *Mich. State U.*
Christine MacIntyre, *Pasadena City College*

FIELD HOCKEY
Caroline Haussermann, *College of William and Mary*

MODERN DANCE
Gay Cheney, *Cal. State at Hayward*
Janet Strader, *Henry St. Playhouse, N.Y.*

WOMEN'S TRACK AND FIELD
Donnis Hazel Thompson, *U. of Hawaii*

SOCCER
Howard Goldman, *Marist College, Poughkeepsie, N.Y.*

SELF-DEFENSE FOR WOMEN
Donald Gustuson, *U. of Hawaii*
Linda Masaki, *Black Belt, Karate*

HANDBALL
John H. Shaw, *Syracuse U.*

FENCING
Maxwell R. Garret, *U. of Ill.*
Mary F. Heinecke, *Lawrence U.*

SKIING
Leonard H. Kalakian, *Mankato State College*
with
Cheryl L. Wayne, *Mankato State College*

ALLYN AND BACON, Inc.
470 Atlantic Avenue
Boston, Mass. 02210

Cade empezó a besarla lentamente, pero un coche interrumpió el ataque. Cade tomó a Abby por la cintura mientras la nube de polvo que había levantado la camioneta se disipaba. Era un viejo modelo.

Travis Randell bajó del coche. La mirada de Travis dejó claro a los ojos de su hermano que había problemas. Los dos fueron a su encuentro.

—Vaya, Travis, ya era hora de que aparecieras —Cade lo abrazó.

—Lo siento. Supongo que debería haber llamado.

Parecía cansado y triste.

—No necesitas llamar. Siempre eres bienvenido. ¿Qué te trae por aquí?

Travis paseó la mirada de uno a otro y luego exhaló un profundo suspiro.

—Echo de menos a mi familia.

Cade estrechó la cintura de su esposa. Así que su hermano pequeño, finalmente había encontrado su camino.

—Supongo que los Randell vuelven a estar juntos —dijo Cade—. Bienvenido a casa, Travis.